Enter the Dialogue

Enter the Dialogue

A Dramatic Approach to Critical Thinking & Writing

Vincent Ryan Ruggiero
STATE UNIVERSITY OF NEW YORK AT DELHI

Wadsworth Publishing Company
Belmont, California
A Division of Wadsworth, Inc.

English Editor: Cedric W. Crocker
Production Editor: Gary Mcdonald
Managing Designer: Paula Shuhert
Designer: Wendy Calmenson
Copy Editor: Susan Thornton
Cover Designer: Wendy Calmenson
Print Buyer: Karen Hunt

Printed in the United States of America
1 2 3 4 5 6 7 8 9 10---89 88 87 86 85

ISBN 0-534-03837-9

Library of Congress Cataloging in Publication Data
Ruggiero, Vincent Ryan.
Enter the dialogue.

Includes index.
1. English language – Rhetoric. 2. Dialogues. 3. Logic.
I. Title.
PE1408.R843 1985 808′.042 84-20900
ISBN 0-534-03837-9

To

LUKE ZILLES,

*Professor Emeritus, SUNY Delhi College,
who was for many years my colleague
and officemate, and whose integrity,
passion for learning, and dedication to
teaching excellence were an inspiration
to me*

Contents

TO THE INSTRUCTOR xi
TO THE STUDENT xv

1 On Dialoguers and Critics: Preliminary Considerations **1**

The Importance of Dialogue, 2
Misconceptions About Dialogue, 2
How Minds Are Conditioned, 4
Where Thinking Goes Wrong, 5
Forms of Self-Deception, 6

Perceiving Selectively, 6
Pretending to Know, 6
Favoring Familiar Views, 7
Face-Saving, 7

Knowing Yourself, 8
Getting Started with Analysis, 8

Writing Tip: Arrange Your Ideas to Achieve Your Purpose, 9
Sample Composition, 10
Dialogue Exercises, 13

2 Reading a Dialogue Critically **18**

The Probability of Error, 19
Recognize and Control Your Bias, 19
The Basic Steps, 20

Understanding Each Side, 21
Identifying the Issue(s), 21
Evaluating the Evidence, 22
Determining Your Position, 23

The Value of a Summary, 25

Writing Tip: Support Your Position with Evidence, 25
Sample Composition, 26
Dialogue Exercises, 28

3 **Making Important Distinctions** 35

Why Distinctions Are Important, 35
Seven Crucial Distinctions, 36

The Distinction Between the Person and the Idea, 36
The Distinction Between Preference and Judgment, 36
The Distinction Between Relevant and Irrelevant Material, 37
The Distinction Between More Important and Less Important Points, 37
The Distinction Between Form and Substance, 38
The Distinction Between Assertion and Evidence, 38
The Distinction Between Familiarity and Validity, 39

Maintaining Objectivity, 39

Writing Tip: Clarify Your Distinctions, 40
Sample Composition, 41
Dialogue Exercises, 43

4 **Recognizing Errors in Reasoning** 50

Looking for Errors, 51
Common Errors in Dialogues, 51

Either-Or Thinking, 51
Stereotyping, 52
Attacking the Person, 52
Contradiction, 53
Faulty Analogy, 53
Faulty Causation, 54
Irrational Appeal, 55
Hasty Conclusion, 56
Overgeneralization, 57
Oversimplification, 57

Avoiding "Fallacy Frenzy," 58

Writing Tip: Clarify Logical Relationships, 59
Sample Composition, 60
Dialogue Exercises, 62

5 **Identifying Assumptions** 70

What Are Assumptions? 71
How Assumptions Affect Reasoning, 71
Some Common Unwarranted Assumptions, 72
Recognizing Specific Assumptions, 74

Writing Tip: Stimulate Your Readers' Interest, 75
Sample Composition, 77
Dialogue Exercises, 78

6 Forming a Judgment **84**

The Necessity of Judgment, 84
How to Form a Judgment, 85

Considering Alternative Arguments, 85
Comparing Arguments and Making a Preliminary Judgment, 87
Assessing Implications and Consequences, 87
Modifying Your Judgment, 88

When to Reserve Judgment, 89

Writing Tip: Express Your Judgment Carefully, 90
Sample Composition, 91
Dialogue Exercises, 93

7 Investigating the Issue **99**

What to Look For, 99

Confirmed Details or Statistics, 100
Your Own Experience and Observation, 100
The Judgments of Authorities, 100
Other People's Experience and Observation, 101

How to Find Evidence, 101

Consult Your Experience and Knowledge, 102
Interview Authorities, 103
Visit the Library, 104

Using the Library Efficiently, 106

Writing Tip: Keep the Emphasis on Your Judgment, 108
Sample Composition, 109
Dialogue Exercises, 111

8 Refining Your Position **117**

Anticipating Others' Reactions, 118
Nine Common Reactions, 119

Writing Tip: Build a Balanced Case, 123
Sample Composition, 124
Dialogue Exercises, 126

More Dialogues for Critical Thinking and Writing **133**

APPENDIX
SOLVING GRAMMATICAL PROBLEMS, 151
A BRIEF GLOSSARY OF USAGE, 156
NOTES, 164
INDEX, 168

To the Instructor

Enter the Dialogue is both an innovation and an invitation. It marks the introduction of the most ancient and efficacious form of philosophical instruction, the dialogue, into the modern teaching of critical thinking and writing. The dialogue is uniquely suited to the needs of contemporary students, many of whom are less comfortable with the written word than students of previous generations. It is a form of discourse that is more familiar to them than the essay, reflecting as it does the casualness, the rapid exchanges, and the spontaneity of everyday conversation. Thus it offers the easiest and most natural way to learn effective thinking.

Even students who have been infected with the notion that all opinions are equally valid, and whose false sense of tolerance prevents them from making a judgment about the most provocative essay, find it hard to resist being drawn into a lively dialogue. *Enter the Dialogue* invites students to make a contribution to the discussion of issues. The numerous dialogues at the ends of the chapters and in the final section of the book provide them an opportunity to develop their intellectual skills by testing other people's arguments for fallacies, checking their own tendencies to self-deception, conducting investigations, weighing evidence, and forming reasonable positions of their own.

Moreover, *Enter the Dialogue* is admirably suited to the teaching of writing because it meets two needs of beginning writers: a sense of urgency and a starting point. The presentation of conflicting views on dozens of timely and timeless issues stimulates students' desire to express their views and eliminates the problem of where to begin by transporting them to the center of each controversy.

Four special features make this book unusually clear and easy for students to use:

1. Each chapter treats one important consideration in critical thinking and one guideline to effective writing.
2. At the end of each chapter a composition is presented to demonstrate the principles and guidelines detailed in the chapter. Each composition is carefully annotated.

3. Each chapter includes a generous number of dialogues for student analysis. These may be used for critical thinking assignments alone, or for critical thinking and composition assignments.
4. A special introduction for students reviews the fundamentals of composition, including the principles of unity, coherence, development, and emphasis, and suggests an efficient approach to writing. This introduction permits the book's chapters to address somewhat more advanced writing concepts and techniques.

Concise enough to be used as a supplemental text, *Enter the Dialogue* may also be used as the sole text in a course. Here is how a chapter might be handled in the latter approach:

Date Due	**Assignment**
Monday	Read Chapter 1. Analyze dialogue exercises 1 and 2. Be prepared to discuss your analyses in class.
Wednesday	Analyze Chapter 1 dialogue exercises 3, 4, and 5. Be prepared to discuss your analyses in class.
Friday	Analyze Chapter 1 dialogue exercises 6, 7, and 8. Be prepared to discuss your analyses in class.
Monday	Choose one of the remaining dialogue exercises in Chapter 1 (9–12). Analyze the dialogue and then write a composition expressing your view. Be sure to follow the guidelines explained in the Introduction and apply the writing tip presented in Chapter 1.

With this approach you would undoubtedly wish to spend more than four classes on certain chapters—for example, Chapter 7, "Investigating the Issue"—and on the special dialogue section at the end of the book.

Enter the Dialogue offers students an additional benefit. Since the dialogues included here are very close in form and substance to those encountered in everyday life and cover the wide range of issues found there, students will find it difficult to resist applying their analytical skills outside the classroom. Critical thinking is thus more likely to be for your students not a sterile textbook procedure to be left behind when they leave your course but a valuable habit of mind to be nurtured throughout their lives.

ACKNOWLEDGMENTS

I wish to express my appreciation to all those who had a part in the making of this book. Special thanks go to John Beard (Olivet College), Don Richard Cox (University of Tennessee), Jimmie Carol Durr (Mississippi State University), Peter Genovese (St. Louis Community College of Meramec), Elizabeth Hanson-Smith (California State University, Sacramento), Nancy W. Johnson (Northern Virginia Community College), and William F. Woods (Wichita State University) for their helpful suggestions; and to Kevin Howat of Wadsworth for his commitment to meaningful innovation in publishing; and to Gary Mcdonald of Wadsworth for his skillful production of the book.

To the Student

This textbook is designed to teach you how to think critically and to express your thoughts in composition form. Its focus, the dialogue, is undoubtedly new to you. The dialogue is used here both to help you understand the principles and techniques of critical thinking and to challenge you to apply your developing intellectual skill to issues that are at this very moment being debated by people around the country and, in many cases, around the world.

To teach you effectively, your instructor must speculate about what you already know (and what you do not know) about critical thinking and composition writing. Chances are he or she reasons as follows:

> Since few high schools teach critical thinking, my students probably know little about the subject. Of course, they may have some skill in thinking, but it is likely to be intuitive and fragmentary. To realize their full thinking potential, they will need a systematic introduction to the principles and techniques of critical thinking. On the other hand, they have studied writing since grade school, so they should have enough competency to skip the basics and focus on slightly more advanced writing considerations. I realize that some may have forgotten what they learned or learned it imperfectly and may therefore need to be reminded of some basic concerns. Nevertheless, I am entitled to have certain expectations for their writing, even for the first compositions they produce in this course.

Such is undoubtedly your instructor's thinking—and it is definitely the thinking of the author of this text. But what specifically are your instructor's expectations? And what steps can you take to ensure that you meet them? The rest of this introduction will answer these important questions.

TEN REASONABLE EXPECTATIONS

Because you have to some extent studied and practiced writing for at least twelve years, your instructor may reasonably expect that you will do the following for each composition you write:

1. *Plan your composition before you write it.* Some people never plan a composition; they just begin writing it. But though they may save fifteen or twenty minutes by using this approach, they usually waste more time than that in false starts. More important, they experience more uncertainty and frustration about their work because they can never be sure they will have enough to say. In planning your compositions, brainstorm the issue and list as many ideas as you can. Then decide what the boundaries of your paper will be—that is, which ideas you will include and which you will exclude.
2. *Select a controlling idea and use it to guide your writing.* It is easy to assume you know exactly what you want to say, but that is seldom the case. Instead, you have a rough notion of what you want to say, a notion you realize is unclear *only when you put it on paper.* (It may take you several revisions to make it exact.) Making your controlling idea precise before you begin your composition will give you a sense of direction and help you decide how to organize your ideas and achieve unity and coherence in your composition.
3. *Have a specific purpose, a clearly stated goal you wish to achieve with your readers.* There are three general purposes in writing: narrative, informative, and persuasive. Often they are used in combination, but in such cases one usually dominates. For most of the writing assignments in this book, persuasion is the sole, or at least the dominant, purpose. By writing down exactly what you expect to accomplish with your readers and reminding yourself of your intention from time to time as you write, you will increase the likelihood of success in achieving that purpose.
4. *Be sensitive to your readers' needs.* Unlike speaking, the writing situation offers your audience no opportunity to overcome confusion about your ideas. They cannot raise their hands and ask what you meant by what you wrote. For that reason you should be alert to any statement that might be misunderstood or misinterpreted, and revise it to minimize that chance.
5. *Be exact and economical in your expression.* To be exact, never settle for a word that is merely close to the meaning you intend. In addition, avoid overly general words such as *great, nice,* and *bad* and overworked expressions such as *couldn't care less, last but not least,* and *a fight to the finish.* (Be suspicious of any expression you have heard others say repeatedly.) To be economical apply these three principles, the first two from George Orwell: Never use a long word where a short word will do; never use a foreign phrase, a scientific word, or a jargon word if you can think of an everyday English equivalent; never use more words than necessary to convey the meaning you intend.

6. *Make your writing lively.* A lively style is not the blessing of a chosen few. Anyone can achieve it by applying two simple strategies. The first is to aim for freshness of perspective. That means eliminating the most predictable ideas from your composition if possible. Predictable ideas are easy to recognize: they are the ones that first come to your mind (and everyone else's). If you can't think of a fresh perspective, or if the common idea is the very best idea, then at least find a fresh way to express or defend it. The other way to make your composition lively is to vary your sentences by combining several short sentences into a longer one or by changing the order of clauses or phrases to vary the sentence beginning.
7. *Break your thoughts into paragraphs.* Effective paragraphs make your compositions easier to read and comprehend. To make your paragraphs effective, be sure they are of moderate length, but sufficiently varied to overcome monotony. Make them average about ten lines. (They may vary from about five to fifteen lines.) In addition, keep your paragraphs unified by eliminating unrelated ideas.
8. *Use standard punctuation.* Properly used punctuation marks assist your readers in comprehending your ideas. Unpunctuated or poorly punctuated passages create confusion and detract from your writing. Many dictionaries contain a brief guide to punctuation.
9. *Observe the conventions of spelling, grammar, and usage.* Errors in spelling, grammar, and usage undermine effective communication of ideas, particularly in persuasive writing, by suggesting that the writer is a careless person. Readers are not likely to place their faith in your reasoning if you demonstrate difficulty grasping basic language conventions that are taught in grade school. It is, of course, no shame to have a problem with such conventions, but it is irresponsible not to take steps to overcome the problem. (To overcome spelling problems, consult a good dictionary and keep a list of the correct spellings of words you have misspelled repeatedly. The Appendix at the end of this book provides a guide to common grammatical errors and a brief glossary of usage.)
10. *Revise your rough draft.* Don't make the mistake of assuming that your first draft is a finished product. The effort required to develop thoughts and keep organization clear makes it impossible for any writer, even a professional, to write and polish at the same time. The time for revision is after the rough draft is completed. The best approach to revising is to read over your rough draft several times, preferably aloud, so that you can hear as well as see its strengths and weaknesses. Revise any part that fails to meet the expectations detailed in points 4 through 9. (Points 1 through 3 concern planning.) Then rewrite the paper, incorporating your revisions.

If you are meticulous in making your writing meet all ten of your instructor's expectations from the outset, you have little reason to worry about your chances for success in this course. All additional writing specifications are explained in the book's chapters, together with sample compositions illustrating how those specifications are applied.

TIME, PLACE, WORKING CONDITIONS

One other consideration is important enough to mention here. To get the most from your efforts in your critical thinking and writing course, you must select the best time, place, and working conditions. No two people respond identically to the same circumstances, so there is no one set of circumstances that suits everyone. Your thinking and writing will proceed much better if you choose the right conditions for you. Are you a morning person, one who functions better at 6:00 A.M. than at 6:00 P.M.? Then try to set aside time early in the morning to do your thinking and writing. Do you work better at a desk or table or in an easy chair? Using a pen, pencil, or typewriter? What conditions best stimulate your thought process? Quiet or noise? Soft music, rock music, or no music? (A word of caution: Just because you *like* Rod Stewart's music does not mean it helps you work better.) Do you work better alone or around others?

If you are not sure what you find stimulating and what you find distracting, experiment and find out. By choosing your working conditions with care, not only will you save time and effort but you will also be more satisfied with the ideas and compositions you produce.

1 On Dialoguers and Critics: Preliminary Considerations

GWEN: It's ridiculous to forbid prayer in the public schools.

GLEN: No, it's not. The Supreme Court ruled against school prayer because it would violate the constitutional separation of church and state.

GWEN: Come on, now. Letting children say "God is great, God is good; let us thank him for our food" is hardly a threat to the separation of church and state. In fact, denying them the opportunity to express their religious belief is a denial of their constitutional freedom to practice religion.

GLEN: You're missing the point. Whenever a teacher leads the class in any activity, that very fact suggests the school endorses the activity. And if the school endorses prayer, that means it favors religion over atheism and agnosticism. That's the same as establishing religion.

GWEN: Wait just a minute. You're wrong when you say. . . .

RECORDED CONVERSATION like the preceding one is called *dialogue.* The earliest form of intellectual commerce, dialogue provided the basis for drama and was one of the first ways of studying philosophy. The dialogues of Plato not only taught innumerable generations of students how to think; they also preserved the ideas of the first great Western thinker, Socrates.

Today, more than two thousand years after Plato, dialogue remains an important part of the intellectual life of most societies. Despite the prominence of reportage and essays in modern newspapers, news magazines, and nonfiction books, most of us devote more time to participating in or observing dialogues than in reading such monologues. We discuss and debate issues with others, and we watch others conversing in our presence, as well as on television and in movies.

THE IMPORTANCE OF DIALOGUE

It is not only because dialogue surrounds us that it is important. It is important, too, because of the way it stimulates our minds. We don't just hear dialogues; we interpret and evaluate them. Even in reading the brief exchange between Gwen and Glen, we raise and answer a number of questions: Which position is more familiar to us? Which statements are factual? Which, if any, are false? Which do we tend to agree with? What is the basis of our agreement? In many cases we handle these questions so quickly and smoothly that we are unaware we are doing so.

Because it is so common and so central in our lives, and because we interpret and evaluate it so readily, dialogue offers a valuable way to study critical thinking. This is not to suggest that every dialogue is productive. Frequently a dialogue will neither illuminate the issue nor lead to its solution. Yet for those skilled in analysis, even an unproductive dialogue can be instructive, revealing people's habits of mind and attitudes, and disclosing what specific errors defeated reasonableness and good sense. Learning the skills of analysis can make us not only better thinkers, but better readers, speakers, and writers as well.

Beginning with Chapter 2 we will examine all the skills required to be proficient in analyzing dialogues. In this chapter, however, we will take an overview of the process. More specifically, we'll examine common misconceptions about dialogue, discuss how people's minds are conditioned and where their thinking goes wrong, and examine the various forms of self-deception they often indulge in. Finally, we'll see how you can improve your self-knowledge and get started with analysis.

MISCONCEPTIONS ABOUT DIALOGUE

The quality of a dialogue depends to a considerable extent on the quality of the ideas and attitudes the dialoguers bring to the task. If those ideas and attitudes are sound and helpful, thinking will be enhanced. If they are flawed, thinking will be flawed. In our time there are four common misconceptions about dialogue. A person seldom harbors all of them at the same time, and they may be present without ever being expressed. Nevertheless, wherever they exist, they undermine the thinking process dialogue depends on. Those misconceptions are as follows:

> ***Misconception 1: That all opinions are equal, so if two people disagree on an issue, both are right. That if people are convinced something is right, then it is right for them.*** **If every opinion were equal, then it would be impossible for anyone to be wrong about anything. Yet everyday experience reveals that mistakes in reasoning are as common as mistakes in arithmetic. Just as**

people can add up a column of figures and get the wrong answer, so they can view a series of facts and draw the wrong conclusion. The degree of conviction people have about their errors in no way lessens the reality of those errors. Moreover, some people develop patterns of thinking that ignore facts in favor of preferences and therefore lead them, with some regularity, into error. To borrow a phrase from Henshaw Ward, these people do not analyze—they THOB. That is, they THink out the Opinion that pleases them, and Believe it.[1]

Misconception 2: That it is a sign of intolerance to disagree with others or to challenge their views. **Tolerance, in the intellectual sense, means willingness to hear and consider thoughtfully views that differ from our own. It does not mean pretending to accept views we do not find acceptable, nor remaining silent when honesty and responsibility compel us to speak out. As long as we express our challenges at appropriate times and in tactful ways, ways that focus on the idea and not on the person who holds it, then disagreement and challenge are perfectly in order.**

Misconception 3: That explanation is justification; in other words, that if a person can explain the reasoning that led to a particular conclusion, then the conclusion must be legitimate. **This misconception confuses understanding and justification. Both are important, and since it is sensible to try to understand before judging, we should pay careful attention to why people think as they do, to the reasoning by which they reach their conclusions. But understanding in no way constitutes justification. Some time ago, for example, a man was arrested for chaining his teenage daughter to a post in the cellar and then burning the house down, killing her. On questioning him, the police determined that the man had been desperately afraid his daughter was prostituting herself and reasoned that if he killed her, she could not bring shame on the family. If understanding equaled justification, the police would have released the man once they learned why he killed his daughter. Happily, they did not release him because, though he definitely had a reason for his action, it was by no means a sufficient one.**

Misconception 4: That the speaker who dominates a dialogue—who says more than others or raises points they can't answer—is thereby the one whose view is correct. **The first part of this misconception is rather transparent. Of course, it would make analysis easier if we could simply count up each person's words and declare the one who spoke most to be the most reasonable. Talkativeness, however, is not synonymous with reasonableness. The second part of this misconception is somewhat more subtle. When people are unable to answer challenges, it often does seem that their positions are deficient. Yet the problem may be with them rather than with their ideas. In other words, there may be a good response to the challenge, but they may either not know it or lack the verbal proficiency to express it. To guard against this misconception, remember that just as the best horse in a race may lose if it is ridden by an incompetent jockey, so a better idea may succumb to an inferior one if it is championed by an incompetent dialoguer.**

HOW MINDS ARE CONDITIONED

We hear a lot about individuality today. Unfortunately, much of what we hear is based on the false notion that everyone's thinking and actions are *necessarily* unique. It is true, of course, that everyone is unique in natural endowments, the talents and capabilities he or she is born with and may choose to develop. But no one exists completely independent of the shaping force of society: no one can avoid being conditioned. For this reason, it is a mistake to think of individuality as something conferred automatically at birth. It must be achieved.

Infants and small children are very pliable. They are molded first by parents and relatives, and later by teachers and friends. They gradually learn, directly and indirectly, what to think about people and situations, what values to honor, and how to react to various kinds of experiences. The habits and attitudes they acquire in this way may be sound and helpful or unsound and harmful. In any case, what they learn becomes deep-seated and difficult to change.

Older children and adolescents are further shaped by a force that can sometimes be even more powerful than that exerted by parents and teachers. That force is popular culture, the ideas and attitudes conveyed by popular books and magazines, television shows, music, and especially advertising. Like clothing and hairstyles, ideas are subject to the whims of fashion, and frequent exposure to even a shallow idea can give it tremendous power over our thinking. Once it crosses the threshold of familiarity, we tend to accept it uncritically. Consider, for example, the phrase "the thrill of victory and the agony of defeat," which most adolescents (and many adults) have heard repeated over and over for years. It is hardly surprising that many people have been influenced by that phrase, and related ones, to believe that winning at all costs is a sane and sensible philosophy.

Another powerful shaping force on adolescent attitudes and behavior is the desire to be accepted by others. (Though this desire exists in childhood and in adulthood as well, it is most closely associated with adolescence because it is usually felt most intensely then.) This desire makes it tempting to conform to group values, doctrines, standards, and expectations. And virtually all groups, even the most noble and honorable, exert at least a subtle pressure on all members to act and speak and even think as they do. It is possible, of course, to find Catholics who openly disagree with their church's position on divorce, National Rifle Association members who openly favor handgun legislation, members of the American Medical Association who publicly declare their belief that doctors are generally overpaid for their services. But they are relatively rare, and understandably so, because standing against one's group is uncomfortable.

Numerous studies have shown that the urge to conform to the group is too powerful for many people to resist. In one famous study each subject was directed to match a line drawn on one card with the line of equal length on another card. (The second card had a number of lines of varying lengths to choose from.) Unbeknown to the subject, all the other participants in the experiment had agreed to choose the wrong line. Thus all subjects had to decide whether to honor their own judgment or to abandon their judgment to agree with the group. Many subjects abandoned their judgment, in some cases even when there was a *seven-inch difference* in length between the lines.[2]

Many people persuade themselves that they are individuals when in fact they are little more than products of their conditioning. We have a right to think of ourselves as individuals only when we have become aware of the influences on us and have gained a significant measure of control over our tendency to yield to them unthinkingly.

WHERE THINKING GOES WRONG

When thinking goes right, people make factual statements that are relevant to the matter being discussed and receive other people's factual, relevant statements openly and without prejudice. In addition, they make sensible interpretations and draw sound conclusions from what is said. That situation, of course, is the ideal, which is seldom achieved because in real-life situations people tend to be less than perfectly rational.

There are three broad kinds of error that occur in dialogue:

Omitting or ignoring important considerations that must be considered to reach a sound conclusion

Misinterpreting or incorrectly evaluating the statements that are made

Drawing invalid conclusions: that is, conclusions that do not logically follow from the evidence presented

One cause of these errors, which even the best thinkers may commit from time to time, is simple carelessness. But there is another, more serious cause: self-deception. Self-deception is the process whereby thinking is dominated by biases, preconceived notions, and personal preferences rather than by evidence and careful judgment. Although every thinker is susceptible to self-deception, good thinkers are more effective than others in guarding against it.

FORMS OF SELF-DECEPTION

Self-deception takes a number of specific forms, four of which are especially common: perceiving selectively, pretending to know, favoring familiar views, and face-saving. Familiarizing yourself with them will help you recognize them when they occur in the dialogues in this book and in everyday life.

Perceiving Selectively

People see and hear things not quite objectively, but filtered through their interests and understanding. For example, three people are walking down a street side by side. The same scene confronts all three, yet the details that dominate the attention of one are little more than an indistinct blur to the others. The first, an artist, focuses on the range of color of people's clothing, the shapes and patterns of store signs, and the arrangements of light and shadow. The second, an engineer, is preoccupied with the structure of the buildings, the kinds of decorative embellishments that give each facade its special character, and the design of the arcades. The third, a physical education instructor, focuses on the way people move, their musculature, the subtle evidence they give of athletic proficiency or lack of it. In each case, the parts of the scene that dominate their attention will be most strongly impressed on their minds and, later, most clearly remembered.

Such focusing is very natural and does not necessarily harm thinking. But when it is influenced by preconceived notions and desires, it can distort people's views of reality. In such cases, people see (and hear) what they want to see or expect to see, instead of what is there. They observe and read distortedly, focusing on details that reinforce their prejudices and ignoring others that challenge those prejudices. Thus people who are prejudiced against blacks and think of them as violent and dishonest will notice and remember reports of violent, dishonest blacks and overlook or quickly forget reports of violent, dishonest whites or of pacific, honest blacks. In time they will have accumulated a memory full of evidence that reinforces their prior beliefs, all of it perceived selectively.

Pretending to Know

People rely on memory when they decide what they know. Memory, unfortunately, is sometimes vague and confused, causing people to believe they know things they do not in fact know. This normal capacity for remembering incorrectly is greatly intensified by deliberately pretending to know. Here's how it works. Someone asks Martin, "Have you ever read Freud?" Knowing that Freud is an important author and not wanting to appear unread, Martin lies, "Yes, I've read Freud." The sentence sinks into his memory. Later, when the question of having read Freud arises again, Martin searches his memory. What then surfaces is not the memory of having said he read Freud, but the memory of having read Freud. Martin's pretense has fashioned reality more to his liking.

A similar problem often arises when people guess or speculate rather than admit "I don't know." For example, someone asks Agnes, "Why did your roommate leave the party early?" Rather than claim ignorance, Agnes guesses, "Oh, she's probably angry at her boyfriend." A week or so later, after her imagination has had time to make its contribution to the self-deception, Agnes "remembers" not only that her roommate was angry but that she confided her feelings to Agnes in detail.

Favoring Familiar Views

People tend to prefer familiar ideas to unfamiliar ones. That is understandable enough. They have developed responses to familiar ideas, so they are confident in dealing with them. Unfamiliar ideas challenge that confidence and make people feel uneasy. The very newness of such ideas makes them strange, unwelcome, suspect. And if they are not only new but also at odds with established notions, they are likely to receive an even less cordial response.

Despite their preference for familiar views, intellectually secure people usually manage to open their minds and give new views a fair hearing, accepting them if they prove worthy, rejecting them if they do not. Insecure people, on the other hand, set about opposing them immediately, often before they fully understand them. They may deceive themselves that they have valid reasons for their opposition, but their only real reason is that the ideas are new to them.

Face-Saving

It is natural for people to want to think well of themselves and to have others think well of them. Most people manage to keep this desire within reasonable bounds and not let it interfere with their evaluation of ideas. Some people, unfortunately, value their self-image or public image more highly than intellectual honesty. They refuse to admit a mistake in thought or in deed, so they practice face-saving. The best-known form of face-saving is shifting the blame onto other people, or fate, or circumstance. In dialogue, however, face-saving usually takes slightly different forms: people claiming their words have been misunderstood (when they haven't) or shifting the focus of the dialogue away from the area of potential embarrassment to them.

Each of the four forms of self-deception may be completely conscious but is more often semiconscious or unconscious. That is why people have such difficulty conquering this problem; like any deeply ingrained bad habit, it frequently occurs without their realizing it. Accordingly, however gross the logical blunders you encounter in the dialogues in this book or in everyday life, remember that they are less likely to be prompted by malice or a lack of regard for the truth than by lack of mental vigilance.

KNOWING YOURSELF

So far we have discussed the problem of self-deception as it occurs in the thinking of others. It is important to recognize that kind of self-deception because it corrupts thinking and prevents dialogue from being productive. Yet it is even more important to recognize our own self-deception. There are two reasons for this: first, because we can know others' self-deception only indirectly, through clues contained in their words and actions, whereas we can know our own directly; secondly, because we can only identify other people's problems, whereas we can conquer our own.

To make rapid progress in becoming an effective thinker, develop the habit of critically examining your reactions to dialogues. Note occasions of your own perceiving selectively, pretending to know, favoring of familiar views, and face-saving. Become so sensitive to fluctuations in your thinking behavior that you anticipate your irrational reactions and take measures to avoid them before they do harm.

GETTING STARTED WITH ANALYSIS

The following approach contains the basic steps necessary for analyzing dialogues. It is the approach you will use in doing the exercises at the end of this chapter. (Subsequent chapters will expand upon this approach.)

1. Read the dialogue carefully, being alert to the developing positions of each person, particularly those offered in response to challenges from the other person(s). Suspend all judgment of the positions and try to keep your impressions very tentative. (Judging too quickly is one of the most common mistakes in analysis.) Your goal in this step is not to agree or disagree, but to understand. If you fail in this goal and misunderstand what is said, your judgment will be flawed.

2. Appraise the strengths and weaknesses of the views expressed. Start by asking these questions about each significant statement made in the dialogue:

If the statement purports to be factual . . .	*IS THE STATEMENT TRUE?*
If the statement presents an interpretation or a judgment . . .	*IS THE INTERPRETATION OR JUDGMENT THE ONLY POSSIBLE ONE? IF IT IS NOT, WHAT ARE THE OTHERS? ARE ANY OF THEM MORE PROBABLE THAN THE ONE PRESENTED?*

However, don't limit yourself to these questions. Ask whatever questions are necessary to probe the reasonableness of the dialoguers' views. And look for hints of self-deception, both in the dialoguers' presentations and in your appraisal. Keep complete notes of the strengths and weaknesses of the views expressed in the dialogue and of your responses to the questions you raised.

3. Decide what overall view of the issue is most reasonable—that is, what view would most successfully withstand all possible objections that might be advanced. This view you select may be one of those expressed in the dialogue, or an entirely different one.

WRITING TIP: ARRANGE YOUR IDEAS TO ACHIEVE YOUR PURPOSE

In every good composition the sentences and paragraphs are so arranged that the message is clear and easy to follow. That kind of arrangement does not happen automatically. In most cases, ideas come to us in random, shopping-list fashion, one triggering another. The fifth idea that occurs to us may be more closely related to the second than to the fourth. That is why effective writers—professionals as well as amateurs—take the time to arrange their ideas before presenting them to others. Here is a simple approach to use in arranging your ideas:

1. Examine all the ideas you listed during your analysis of the dialogue. Decide whether your purpose in writing should be merely to demonstrate the errors of one or both of the dialoguers or to demonstrate the errors and present a more reasonable view of the issue. Note: Whenever mere demonstration of errors leaves the larger issue unresolved, it is your responsibility to address that issue unless you lack the necessary knowledge to do so; and in that case you should explain what knowledge is required for the issue to be resolved. (For example, if the issue centered around the statement "Mermaids must exist because people over the centuries have claimed to see them," you would show

the error of that reasoning and then discuss the reasonableness of believing in mermaids.)

2. Study your list of ideas to decide what arrangement will most effectively achieve the purpose you decided on in step 1 above. Don't assume that the order in which the ideas occurred to you is the most effective order—it seldom is. Consider different possibilities and then number the ideas in the order you decide is best. Follow this decision in writing your composition.
3. If, in studying your list, you find a gap in your thinking, add whatever ideas are necessary to close the gap.

There are a number of patterns of organization that can be used, singly or in combination, in compositions that analyze issues. The most important of these are the following:

Evidence-to-Conclusion Order: The evidence that led to your conclusion is presented first, then the conclusion itself.

Cause-to-Effect (Effect-to-Cause) Order: Cause-to-effect order first states a phenomenon (for example, the Great Depression) and then discusses the effects that resulted from it. Effect-to-cause order begins with the effect (for example, the social revolution of the 1960s) and then discusses the causes. To decide which order to use, consider what is in dispute. If the cause is in dispute, begin with the effect, and vice versa.

Order of Complexity: The simpler aspects of the issue are dealt with first, and then the more complex ones. In most cases, the complex ones are given closer attention.

Order of Importance: The ideas are arranged according to their relative importance, the most important coming last. If the issue is highly controversial, however, the order is slightly modified, the most important idea coming last, and the second most important coming first. This arrangement is designed to give the readers both a good first impression and a good last impression.

SAMPLE COMPOSITION

To illustrate how the basic steps to analysis and the writing tip on arranging your ideas apply, here is the complete process, beginning with the dialogue.

The Dialogue | **The Questions**

LUCINDA: Boris, you're a dangerous driver. You take chances you shouldn't take.

BORIS: Don't sweat it, Luci. I know what I'm doing. I've never had an accident.

Can a person never have had an accident and yet be a dangerous driver?

LUCINDA: What about the time last month when you went off in the ditch after you lost control of the car on the curve?

BORIS: I meant I had no real accidents. That time I just dented the fender a bit and scraped up the side of the car. I wasn't even shaken up.

Is this distinction between accidents and "real" accidents a valid one? Or is this a case of self-deception?

LUCINDA: Another thing I don't like is the drinking and driving—worse yet, the drinking while driving. How can you justify that to anyone, even to yourself?

BORIS: I don't want a big hassle over it, but I know you care about me, so I'll explain how I feel. It may sound silly to you, but I believe we all die when our time comes, not one second sooner. If it's not my time, then I won't die, no matter how drunk I am behind the wheel or how hard I romp on the accelerator. Now let's change the subject.

What does "when our time comes" mean? That one's time and manner of death are foreordained? That it is impossible for a person to do anything to hasten his or her death? How reasonable is such an interpretation?

The writer's purpose: Since the issue here is whether Boris's driving habits can be justified by his particular brand of fatalist philosophy, there is no reason for the writer to address any larger issue, such as "Is fatalism in any of its forms a reasonable philosophy?" The writer's purpose is therefore merely to show the unreasonableness of Boris's view.

The notes: The numbering shows the arrangement that the writer decided would serve the composition's purpose most effectively. (Crossed-out notes were judged to be repetitious or irrelevant.)

2 What would sensible people say causes death in accidents? The laws of physics, the frailty of the human body.

~~Need cases where death caused by own behavior, not by fate.~~

5 A person falling out of a plane.

1 A person jumping from a tall building.

3 Boris would probably say it was fate in these cases.

6 Alcoholics drinking themselves to death; organs often prove they've hurt themselves.

7 No, he'd still say fate.

4 It's hard to answer him.

~~What about the effects of his drinking and driving on other people?~~

12 He doesn't really care about others, just does as he pleases.

8 Boris's view is shallow and self-serving.

9 Responsible people, including fatalists, don't think only of themselves.

11 They think of other drivers and pedestrians.

10 They teach their children to be careful, to look before crossing streets, to look before diving into the swimming pool.

The Composition

Thinking of Others

Distraught and seeing no reason to go on living, the man climbs out a seventy-fifth floor window of the skyscraper and lunges forward, plummeting to the pavement below. Will he survive the fall? Most people would consider the laws of physics and the fact that the human body is not built for sudden, high-velocity rendezvous with concrete and conclude that the man's death is almost certain. Boris, however, would disagree. For him the most important consideration would not be physics, but destiny.

It is not as easy to answer Boris's argument as it might seem. We could, of course, choose a more dramatic example, like that of a person falling thirty thousand feet from a plane without a parachute. But Boris would very likely answer that people have been known, however rarely, to survive such experiences. Or we could point out that thirty-five-year-old victims of chronic alcoholism have been found to have the organs of eighty-year-olds, a clear indication that they hastened their own deaths. Yet Boris would undoubtedly reply that it was their fate to die in such condition.

Such arguments do not effectively answer Boris's view because he has every eventuality covered. If the person dies, then he was destined to die; if he doesn't, then he wasn't.

The real error in Boris's argument is not that it is fatalistic, but that it is shallow and self-serving. Responsible fatalists do not let their view of nature endanger other people's lives. They teach their children to look both ways before crossing the street and to check to be sure there is water in the pool before diving in. Even more to the point, responsible fatalists, like all conscientious citizens, refuse to mix drinking and driving or to drive recklessly, because they acknowledge the rights of other drivers and pedestrians and their own responsibility to honor those rights.

Unlike responsible fatalists, Boris thinks only of himself, saying, in effect, "I'll do as I please and let the consequences fall where they may." The great weakness in that view is that it takes no account of other people.

DIALOGUE EXERCISES

Analyze each of the following dialogues as explained in "Getting Started with Analysis," page 8. Then write a composition on one of them, applying the writing tip given at the end of the chapter.

1 ______________________________

BETTY: Did you hear the news? The Dean just approved the request of the Gay Rights Caucus. From now on, homosexual couples will be allowed to attend all campus dances.

BRUNO: I'm not surprised. He's probably a fag himself. He certainly walks like one. But now he's gone too far.

BETTY: He said in his open letter to students that a college campus is a place for tolerance and open-mindedness and that gays have the same rights as anyone else.

BRUNO: Yeah? Well, I have rights too. And when I can't dance with my woman without being surrounded by whirling weirdos, then my rights are being violated. If I pay for my ticket, I shouldn't have to have my stomach upset.

2 ______________________________

DAD: [Commenting on his teenage son's latest stereo tape] How can you listen to that garbage? It sounds like primal therapy hour at the county asylum.

LAD: Here we go again. If you tried to understand my generation's music, you'd see it's not so bad.

DAD: What's to understand? Half the time the words are unintelligible, and the other half they're so nonsensical that you wish they were unintelligible. In my day . . .

LAD: Spare me, please. I know it by heart. In your day songs were sung clearly by graduates of public speaking programs and lyrics were profoundly meaningful and inspiring.

DAD: Something like that, yes.

3 ______________________________

Note: On a trip to Spain in November 1982, Pope John Paul acknowledged that the Spanish Inquisition, which occurred in 1483 and resulted in two thousand people's being imprisoned, tortured, and burned at the stake, was a mistake.[3]

RALPH: It's about time the Catholic church officially condemned the Inquisition.

CHESTER: The pope shouldn't have admitted that publicly.

RALPH: Why? Do you think five hundred years after the fact is too soon? Should he have waited for one thousand years to pass?

CHESTER: Don't be sarcastic. I mean that his statement will undoubtedly weaken the faith of many Catholics. If you love someone or something—in this case, the church—you should do nothing to cause it shame or embarrassment. Of course the Inquisition was wrong, but it serves no good purpose to say so now and remind people of the church's error.

4 ______________________________

RAY: I'm telling you that UFOs exist! When you add up all the sightings by various people all over the world, you can't come to any other conclusion.

SADIE: If UFOs existed, scientists and military experts would have captured one by now and reported on it.

RAY: Not necessarily. If they are piloted by beings of advanced intelligence, they can easily evade capture. And anyway, how do you know the authorities haven't captured one already and kept the fact secret so people wouldn't panic?

SADIE: I just know they don't exist. People are so easily deceived—they see what they want to see, or what science fiction has conditioned them to see. Their imagination plays tricks on them.

5 ______________________________

ERNA: Did you read that magazine article about Brenda Vavoom, the soap opera star? It said she's divorcing her husband so she can marry her co-star, Randy Wrangle.

VERNA: Yeah, I read it, but I also heard on today's news that she denies both that she's planning a divorce and that she's having an affair with Wrangle. In fact, she says she's going to sue the magazine for defamation of character.

ERNA: I heard that too, but it's obvious she's lying. What possible reason would the magazine have for printing a false story? If she were innocent, they wouldn't have written about her. What's that old saying—"Where there's smoke, there's fire."

6 ______________________________

Note: A Roswell, New Mexico, woman shot her former husband, then flagged down a passing motorist and demanded at gunpoint that he drive her to a store. There she took several packages of cigarettes at gunpoint and fled. She was charged with aggravated assault, kidnapping, and armed robbery. The judge who heard her case decided she should be rehabilitated in college rather than in prison. He put her on probation, requiring that she attend classes at a nearby college and that she undergo psychiatric treatment. The assistant district attorney who prosecuted her case quit his job in protest over the decision.[4]

ZELDA: That judge's decision is a perfect example of what's wrong with our criminal justice system today—it treats criminals too leniently.

SCOTTIE: I disagree. It was a creative decision. In prison she'd only have been further corrupted. She's obviously a disturbed person. College and therapy will help her get her life in order.

ZELDA: But everybody who commits a crime can be said to be disturbed if we stretch the term enough. If the courts go out of their way to avoid sending people to prison, criminals will be encouraged to commit crimes.

7 ______________________________

BOBBI JO: You know, my Asian cultures course has changed my mind about marriage.

BILLY BOB: How so?

BOBBI JO: Traditionally, most Asian cultures have arranged young people's marriages. The parents would decide which boy would marry which girl. The kids themselves would have no choice in the matter. Many times they wouldn't even have met each other until the time of the wedding.

BILLY BOB: That's terrible. It leaves love and mutual attraction out of it altogether. How can they possibly know they're compatible unless they learn all about each other first and then decide whether they belong together?

BOBBI JO: I know it sounds odd when you first hear it. But it really makes good sense. Parents are older and tend to choose more sensibly. Anyway, history has proved the wisdom of the practice. Divorce is virtually unknown in those cultures.

8 ______________________________

Note: After working twelve years for the federal government in one California town, a woman was transferred to an office job in a nearby town. Many of the workers in the office smoked. Immediately, the woman began experiencing chest pains, congestion, and breathing difficulty. Doctors blamed her exposure to cigarette smoke and recommended that she not return to work. She applied for disability but was denied it. After a long court battle, the U.S. Court of Appeals awarded her $20,000 in retroactive payments and said she must either be provided a smoke-free environment to work in within sixty days or be made eligible for disability pay of $500 per month.[5]

IVAN: Hooray. The right of nonsmokers to breathe unpolluted air is finally being recognized.

URSULA: Sorry to burst your bubble, but the decision was unfair. If she couldn't stand the conditions in the office, she should have quit and gotten a job with more favorable conditions. The court's decision penalizes the other employees for her medical problem. If this legal precedent is allowed to stand, every troublemaker who dislikes cigarettes can just complain, and others will be denied their right to smoke.

9 ______________________________

ACE: Charlie, did you play football in high school?

CHARLIE: I was on the team for four years, but I can't say I really played. I saw about two minutes of playing time twice a year. The rest of the time I warmed the bench.

ACE: It doesn't really matter how much you played. It's being on the team, sharing the spirit that counts. You learn things about yourself you can't learn in any other way. You become a man.

CHARLIE: There's some truth in what you say, but mostly it's a lot of crap. I learned about myself, all right. I learned that I was capable of wishing the first-stringers would suffer crippling injuries so I'd get a chance to play. I learned how to feel, and be, second-rate. And I learned how to be a phony and cheer for my teammates when I really felt only anger and envy.

ACE: If you had been a real team player, you wouldn't have had those feelings.

10 ______________________________

Note: After a high school student in Milpitas, California, raped and murdered his former girlfriend and threw her body into a ravine, he boasted of his crime to friends and took some of them to see the girl's remains. One friend kicked leaves and bags over the body. For that action he was charged with being an accessory after the fact of murder and sentenced to three years at a ranch for delinquent boys.[6]

MAUDE: Good. The creep got what he deserved.

CLAUDE: I disagree. Of course, what he did was insensitive, but not really an evil act. The girl was already dead. He couldn't bring her back to life. So kicking leaves over her body did no harm.

MAUDE: Kicking the leaves was helping to conceal the crime. He should have reported the murder to the police.

CLAUDE: That's an unreasonable demand. The murderer was his friend. Telling on him would have been an act of disloyalty.

11 ______________________________

CLARISSA: [Flipping the TV dial and not finding anything to her liking] Nothing but situation comedies again. I refuse to watch that drivel. It really ought to be banned.

SYLVESTER: Clarissa, you're a snob. If people don't share your taste, you think there's something wrong with them. There are millions of people in this country who love situation comedies. You can't expect the networks to reflect your views only.

CLARISSA: I'm not saying that everyone should share my taste. But let's face it, there are levels of taste. And the level of people who love situation comedies is subhuman.

SYLVESTER: What an outrageous statement. When are you going to learn that no person's taste is better than anyone else's. It's a free country, so we all have a right to like whatever we choose.

12 ______________________________

Analyze the dialogue about prayer in the schools on the first page of this chapter.

2 Reading a Dialogue Critically

ETHEL: Cal Thomas, the Moral Majority's vice president for communications, says a subtle kind of discrimination is being practiced against religious conservatives in the United States.[1]

FRED: That doesn't surprise me. The Moral Majority is always complaining about something.

ETHEL: He says religious books are rarely reviewed in newspapers and magazines or on network television. He cites the example of a book by Dr. Francis Shaeffer that outsold Jane Fonda's exercise book 300,000 to 150,000 one month; yet her book made number one on the *New York Times* best-seller list, and his wasn't even mentioned.

FRED: So what. Those guys are all for censorship. They have no business objecting when someone censors their books.

EFFECTIVE READING means more than seeing words. It means understanding, too. And critical reading means still more: careful evaluation of what is read. Too often we read a sentence or two and some word or phrase triggers an association in our minds so absorbing that we neglect both understanding and evaluation. That may have happened to you when you read the dialogue above. You may have read the words *Moral Majority* and thought "Who are they to speak for everyone else? I resent their making pronouncements about so many issues. They seem to be browbeating me into affirming their views. Maybe that bumper sticker I saw recently—'The Moral Majority is Neither'—is true." In other words, your eyes were reading, but your mind was not.

Whenever our attention is diverted in this way (and it can happen when our reaction is positive as well as when it is negative), our evaluation of the dialogue is almost certain to be badly flawed. How can any analysis be worth much when it consists of ignoring the idea and focusing on something else! The first step in reading a dialogue, then, is to control the tendency to think of something else and to concentrate on the dialogue itself.

THE PROBABILITY OF ERROR

The next step in becoming a critical reader is to appreciate the commonness of error. All of us are subject to a variety of errors. We may perceive inaccurately, remember incorrectly, misunderstand others' statements, misinterpret the data of our experience, draw invalid conclusions, and misstate our views. Such errors are part of the human condition and no one can ever escape them completely. However many degrees a person may have, however great his or her level of expertise, the danger of error is always present. And in dialogue, which often involves disagreement over matters of conviction, the danger is heightened.

As a critical reader, you must expect to find error in whatever you read. That does not mean you must be a nitpicker, calling attention to every minor flaw you see, so busy finding tiny errors that you lose sight of the larger matters. Rather, it means that you must be alert to the imperfection that is a natural part of human discourse. That alertness will help you not only to identify weaknesses in arguments, but also to recognize strengths and to discriminate between arguments of slightly differing quality.

RECOGNIZE AND CONTROL YOUR BIAS

It is possible to approach an issue without bias. But that seldom happens. And you can be sure that it won't in any situation where you have strong feelings about the issue. Not that there is anything wrong with having strong feelings. After all, it is not only proper but desirable to have convictions, to favor the sides of issues that reflect your principles. What is wrong is pretending that such feelings do not constitute a bias, that you can disregard them and still be objective. Such pretense undermines critical thinking.

Reading a dialogue critically is very much like walking a high wire in a circus act. Though the journey may seem to be perfectly straight, in fact it is composed of hundreds of subtle corrections. Aerialists sense a slight leaning to the right or left and imperceptibly shift the weight of the balancing bar to compensate. The greater the leaning, the greater the shift. Avoiding a fall depends on the acuteness of their sense of balance—that is, how quickly they realize which way they are leaning and how far—and on the quickness of their efforts to compensate. It is the same in critical thinking. You must realize when you are leaning to one side and consciously make yourself regain your balance. Later, when you have completed an open-minded reading of the dialogue and given a fair hearing to each point of view, you can decide whether the evidence supports one side more than the other.

Let's examine an excerpt from a dialogue and see how this effort to offset bias takes place:

ALICIA: I read recently that a publisher has sued a university photocopying center and several faculty members for reproducing copyrighted material without the authors' or publishers' permission. I think that's terrible. Today's publishers seem motivated only by greed and have no regard for education and the intellectual life.

ROBIN: Are you sure their case had no merit? Maybe the copying did infringe copyright.

ALICIA: Nonsense. All their so-called reasons for objecting were a cover for their greed. . . .

It's almost impossible for anyone associated with education in any way to read this excerpt without having some feelings about the issue. Some students and professors would lean heavily toward Alicia's view *even before completing the first sentence.* (Many textbook authors and publishers, of course, would lean the opposite way.) How does that leaning threaten critical thinking? By leading them to prejudgment. Before Robin utters a word, they are predisposed to be suspicious of, or downright hostile toward, what she says. Similarly they are likely to be predisposed to accept whatever Alicia says, even if it does not make good sense. Unless such predispositions are controlled, fair reading is impossible.

Here is a technique you can use to become more aware of your biases and to prevent them from undermining your critical reading. During your first reading of a dialogue, get actively involved, but not as a disputant; rather, as an impartial, inquisitive third party. Write appropriate questions in the margins. Whenever you find yourself making a statement instead of raising a question or questioning one side but not the other, realize that you are showing bias and make an effort to be critical of both sides. Your questions will have the additional value of providing a framework for the judgment and response you will make later.

THE BASIC STEPS

Chapter 1 presented a simple approach to analyzing dialogues. Let's now expand that approach, looking more closely at the requirements of critical reading and thinking. We'll examine four steps: understanding each side, identifying the issue(s), evaluating the evidence, and determining your position.

Understanding Each Side

There can be no responsible judgment of an idea unless the idea is first understood. This may seem too obvious to say. Yet the unfortunate fact is that it is often overlooked. People judge others' views before they have heard them fully expressed. What they are judging in such cases is not the views themselves, but some stereotyped notion of the views that exists in their minds. (Some people even betray that fact by saying "Don't bother to go on; I know what you are going to say.") This approach is especially offensive when it is used with careful thinkers. For such people recognize complexity and deal with it effectively; their views are seldom fairly represented by stereotypes.

The great enemy of understanding others' views is preoccupation with our own views. How many times have you heard someone barely begin explaining her view and then found yourself slipping off into a silent recitation of your own view. Someone may say, for example, "I think grading is too lenient at this college because . . . ," and while she continues her explanation, you are saying to yourself, "She's wrong; most professors are too rigorous in their grading. For example . . ." Then a minute or two later, when it is your turn to speak, you offer what you have been thinking as a challenge to her view, even though you never heard and therefore cannot be sure you understand her view. The same process can occur when you are reading a dialogue.

To improve your understanding of others' views, forbid yourself from preoccupation with your own thoughts while you are reading. (If an insight occurs to you that is too important to set aside, stop reading long enough to jot it down; then return to reading, giving your full attention to what is said.) Aim to grasp each dialoguer's line of thought. Try to enter his consciousness, see the issue as he does, adopt his perspective. Pay special attention to the connections between his thoughts: the "becauses" he cites. Do all this even if the dialoguer's view is shallow or absurd.

In the beginning this approach may seem to represent abandoning your own ideas and convictions and embracing alien views. It may even seem an insult to your individuality. It is not. Understanding a view is not the same as endorsing it. The better you understand all views, the more effectively you can reason out and defend your own view later.

Identifying the Issue(s)

Critical reading allows no room for vagueness. If we do not have a clear conception of what the issue is, we can hardly expect to evaluate the opposing arguments effectively. Identification, however, is not always an easy task. Consider, for example, this excerpt from a dialogue:

CARL: At last there is a way to administer capital punishment that is humane: the lethal injection. The subject is first given an anesthetic, then a muscle relaxant, and then a drug to stop the heart.

DAVE: You're kidding yourself. Any form of capital punishment is barbaric. However neat and painless they make it, it still represents society's taking vengeance, and that's hypocritical.

CARL: That's an unrealistic view. Capital punishment is the only real deterrent to crime. Furthermore, society has no obligation to provide food, clothing, and shelter to those who prey on it. Convicts under life sentences are a terrible financial burden.

Even in this short passage there are no fewer than three separate issues: Is capital punishment morally objectionable? Is it a deterrent to crime? And is the cost of maintaining convicts for life a "terrible financial burden"? As the dialogue continues, even more issues may emerge. Of course, not all the issues will necessarily be of equal importance. In many cases, there will be only one main issue, with the rest being subordinate to it. But no matter what the case, it is important to recognize what the issues are, to sort them out and determine their interrelationships and relative importance.

To identify the issue(s) in dialogue effectively, be alert for two kinds of disputes: what is so and what ought to be. The former concerns matters of fact; the latter, matters of judgment. When you are first reading the dialogue, mark both kinds. Later, review the passages you have marked and decide the relationship between the disputes and the relative importance of each. Then write down briefly what the central issue is. (If there are two or more central issues, write each down.) This written statement will be a valuable aid to analyzing the dialogue and making a judgment. It is especially helpful in the case of extended and complex dialogues, where the potential for confusion is greater.

Evaluating the Evidence

In the broadest sense, evidence is anything that is offered to support a point of view. (In this sense, it is possible to have shallow, illogical, and therefore unacceptable evidence.) Our focus will be on a slightly more restricted definition: anything that may *reasonably* be offered in support of a point of view.

It is important to differentiate between evidence and proof. Proof is a final state in which there is no room for doubt because the evidence is so compelling as to settle all questions. That state seldom exists. Even when issues are resolved, they usually lack such finality. It is therefore most sensible to regard few, if any, issues as settled, and to think in terms of evidence rather than proof, particularly in relation to our own views. In so doing, we are more likely to be sensitive to the possible objections others might have to our positions.

There are four broad kinds of evidence: independently confirmed details or statistics, your own experience and observation, the judgments of authorities, and other people's experience and observation. Though they may differ in quality, all four kinds of evidence are valuable.* Nevertheless, they are all subject to error. In evaluating a dialogue, you should therefore not take the evidence at face value. If the evidence is someone's experience or observation, consider whether it is first-hand (that is, the speaker's own), or second- or third-hand. Even first-hand perception can be flawed by preconceptions and inattention, and when a report is filtered through several minds, distortion is likely.

Remember, too, that when people present their experiences and observations, they are seldom presenting the details alone; they are including their interpretations and judgments about those details. Accordingly, much of what is offered as factual material is colored by the degree of expertise, fairness, and reasonableness of the individual offering it. These qualities are often lacking in many individuals. (Note that calmness is not necessarily a sign of reasonableness. A speaker may be highly emotional and yet offer a reasonable argument.)

There is one additional consideration to be made in evaluating a dialogue: what is omitted. The participants will often feel passionately for their views, so they can be expected to be limited in perspective. In addition, the give and take of dialogue seldom permit the full development of an argument. A point that one has in mind at the beginning may be forgotten in the course of discussion and never be expressed. The reader thus may get only a fragmentary picture of the issue. In such cases, before you can reach a fair judgment of the issue, you must consider not only the evidence that is presented, but also the evidence that is intentionally or unintentionally omitted.

In summary, evaluating the evidence in a dialogue consists of asking and answering these questions: Are the details or statistics offered by the dialoguers independently confirmed? What is the likelihood that the experiences and observations offered are reliable representations of what happened? How expert, fair, and reasonable are the dialoguers' judgments? What important evidence, if any, has been omitted?

Determining Your Position

The fourth and final step is to decide what your position is on the issue. This does not mean remembering what you were taught as a child or what

* The kinds of evidence are dealt with more fully in Chapter 7.

you heard your peers saying about the issue. Nor does it mean recalling what you have always thought. It means deciding what the most reasonable view is in light of all the evidence you have considered.

It will not always be easy to treat your own position as critically as you do the positions of others, particularly if you feel strongly about an issue. Familiarity is the enemy of objectivity. Nevertheless, it is necessary to be critical of your position. If you are not, if you merely restate your old view without subjecting it to the same scrutiny you practice with other views, then all your efforts to understand the dialoguers' views, to identify the issue, and to evaluate the evidence will have been a waste of time.

The following guidelines will help you determine your position effectively. (Chapter 6 treats the matter of judgment in detail.)

1. Don't settle for the first judgment that comes to mind. Compare that judgment with a number of others before deciding. Keep in mind that you do not have to agree with one of the dialoguers. Instead, you may agree partly with each or disagree with both.

2. If the evidence does not point conclusively to one judgment, choose the judgment that seems most probable. Some people believe incorrectly that unless the evidence is conclusive, no judgment is legitimate. Defenders of cigarette smoking, for example, often argue that because it has not yet been clinically established that smoking causes cancer and other diseases, it cannot be concluded that smoking is harmful to one's health. That argument is unsound. As long as the evidence is sufficient to support a judgment of what is probable, such a judgment is perfectly legitimate. (Of course, you should remain open to new evidence in such cases and be ready to revise your view in light of whatever new evidence may arise.)

3. Resist the temptation to think of complex issues in oversimplified terms. An action or a line of thought may be less than perfect and yet be the only reasonable one under the circumstances. For example, shooting another person to death can hardly be called a "good" act. Yet if it occurs in the context of self-defense during an attack on one's life, it cannot reasonably be called a "bad" act. To overcome the temptation to think of complex issues in oversimplified terms, don't classify actions or arguments in simple good-versus-bad terms. Instead, decide where they fit on the following scale:

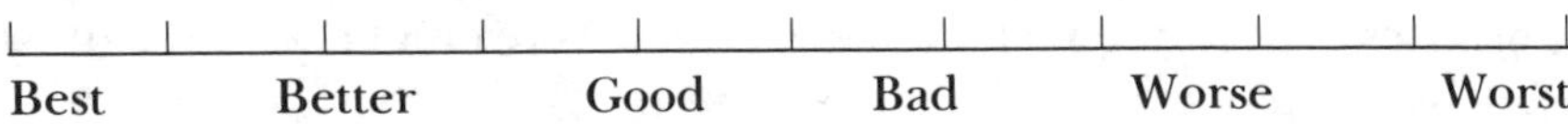

THE VALUE OF A SUMMARY

In dealing with extended or unusually complex dialogues, it is helpful to use a summary of the dialoguers' positions. This involves your stating each dialoguer's view in the briefest form possible without distorting it. The general form for this would be "Alicia believes . . . because. . . ." The advantage of making such a summary is that it reduces the issue to essentials and focuses it more clearly.

How will you know when to use a summary? The first sign is when you find yourself getting confused as the dialogue progresses or forgetting the dialoguers' positions.

WRITING TIP: SUPPORT YOUR POSITION WITH EVIDENCE

When you present evidence to support your views, you provide a guide for other people through unfamiliar territory, the domain of your impressions, feelings, thoughts, and understandings. You recreate for them what you have experienced and observed and learned. Thus you provide a basis for them to accept your judgments. It is as foolish to offer conclusions without evidence as it is to say to someone, "I have added up a dozen numbers and arrived at a total of 32,456. Please endorse it as the right answer." The person would very likely respond, "If you want me to endorse it as the right answer, give me the dozen numbers and let me see if they add up to your total." To expect others to accept your unsupported calculations of reality is to expect them to consider you incapable of error. That is not a reasonable expectation.

The key to providing evidence is to be sensitive to where ideas need to be supported and developed. If you are speaking, your listeners can ask, "Can you provide an example?" or "What leads you to that conclusion?" If you are writing, however, your readers remain silent. The solution to this problem is to ask your own questions (and then answer them). Here's how to use this approach:

Whenever you make an assertion of fact (stating that something is so), ask yourself, "Where did I get that information and how do I know it is accurate? Is the information sufficient? If so, how do I know? If not, what other information might I add?"

Whenever you make an assertion of interpretation or judgment, ask yourself, "How do I know that this interpretation or judgment is the best one possible? And how can I most effectively demonstrate its reasonableness to readers who may be skeptical?"

Your answers to these questions will provide the evidence you need to support your assertions and make your argument persuasive to your readers. As for the specific writing techniques to be used in developing your supporting material, consider the following ones:

Present important details of relevant research studies.

Relate experiences and observations (your own or others') that support your view.

Cite situations, cases in point, in which your ideas apply and explain how they apply. (If appropriate, add descriptive detail to make them dramatic.)

Compare your interpretations and judgments with others and demonstrate their superiority.

Briefly explain the historical background of the issue. (Be sure to limit such explanation to particularly relevant details.)

Identify the causes and effects of problems related to the issue and demonstrate how your view makes their solution easier.

Paraphrase or quote the judgments of authorities that reinforce your judgments.

In writing your responses to the dialogues, remember that whenever you make an assertion, you assume the burden of proof. (*Proof* is used here in the sense of "evidence.") And the more unusual and less obvious your assertions are, the greater that burden is. It is not up to your readers to refute your assertions; it is up to you to substantiate them. If you fail to do so, you should not be surprised when your readers are unpersuaded.

SAMPLE COMPOSITION

Here is a sample composition, together with the dialogue that prompted it, demonstrating the use of evidence to support a position:

The Dialogue	**The Questions**
EMORY: My professor said there's a growing movement to tighten standards in the nation's schools. On top of that he said he agrees with the movement. Can you believe it?	*Is there such a movement? What standards, specifically, are believed to need tightening?*

CORNELIA: Well, maybe it'd be a good thing if standards were tightened. The situation at my school was permissive, and a lot of my friends say the same about their schools.

Would it be a good thing? Exactly what benefits, if any, would it bring about?

EMORY: If anything, the standards are too tight already. Most high schools are like prisons. The teachers and administrators are the guards and the students are the inmates.

Are the standards too tight or too loose? In what way?

The Composition

Welcome Back, Standards

"School should . . . be a place where tolerance toward others is learned, where respect for achievement is nurtured, where self-discipline is attained, and where a child acquires . . . a sense of participation in a society larger than himself." That sentence may sound like a nineteenth century handbook of education, but it's not. It's from a *Life* magazine article of a few years ago, entitled "A Call for Quality Education."[2] Written by a former high school teacher, that article is just one example of the growing dissatisfaction with permissiveness in the nation's schools.

This paragraph provides evidence that some knowledgeable people are calling for a tightening of standards. It also suggests the specific aims that are being recommended, aims the author of this paper is endorsing.

As a college student not long out of high school I share that dissatisfaction. I believe that teachers do students a disservice when they assign no homework, tolerate lateness and inattention, and give B's and A's for substandard performance. And when they allow students to call them by their first names, they invite disrespect.

Apparently many students feel the same way I do. Some even support *dress codes.* For a number of years K. Marshall Clayton, a California high school teacher, has surveyed student and teacher attitudes toward mandatory dress codes. Most of the teachers and many of the students surveyed regard such codes favorably. They express the belief that both student behavior and academic performance would improve with the imposition of a dress code.

This paragraph offers evidence that the call for standards enjoys support from many teachers and students.

I'm not sure I would go so far as to impose dress codes in schools. But I definitely believe there should be more required courses; more homework; more demand that students master such basic skills as spelling, grammar, arithmetic, and penmanship; and tighter graduation standards. In short, I believe there should be less self-discovery and more self-improvement.

Is such a view an overreaction? Has the more indulgent approach to education been given a fair chance? Andrew Nelson, dean of the liberal arts division of this college, answers these questions this way: "Permissiveness has been tried and found wanting. It has produced students who lack the attitudes, values, and basic competencies to succeed in either the academic world or the world of work. The necessary reform is not coming a moment too soon."

In the final paragraph, the author strengthens her case by letting an authority answer the questions, rather than answering them herself. (Though such handling could in some circumstances be an evasion of her responsibility as a writer, in this case it is not because she lacks the competency to answer the questions effectively.)

DIALOGUE EXERCISES

Analyze each of the following dialogues, using the four steps explained in the chapter: that is, understand each side, identify the issue(s), evaluate the evidence, and determine your position. Be sure to recognize and control your biases and to consider using a summary if you experience confusion. Then write a composition on one of the dialogues, presenting and supporting your view and applying the writing tip given at the end of the chapter.

1 ______________________________

AARON: You know, I really believe that cows think.

JENNIFER: That's ridiculous. Animals can't think.

AARON: No, I really mean it. If you've ever watched a cow carefully, you'll know what I mean. I've ridden by them on my bike and they follow my every move as I go by. I've also stood and studied the way they stare off into space. They are more philosophical in their manner than many people.

JENNIFER: None of that establishes that they can think.

AARON: The idea is not as strange as you make out. In India cows are considered sacred.

JENNIFER: Next thing you'll be suggesting is that they teach college courses.

AARON: Don't resort to mockery. If you can't disprove my theory, then you have to admit its validity.

2 ______________________________

Note: A Rochester, New York, lawyer has issued a court challenge to the practice of charging women half-price for drinks during "ladies' nights" at bars. He argues that the practice is a form of sex discrimination against men.[3]

HENRIETTA: That lawyer must be making a joke against feminism. He can't be serious.

BURT: Why not? It's clearly a case of discrimination.

HENRIETTA: Look, we both know why ladies' nights are scheduled in bars: as a gimmick to attract customers. The women flock to the bars to get cheap drinks, and the men flock there because the women are there. It's no different from other gimmicks, such as mud-wrestling contests and "two for the price of one" cocktail hours.

BURT: Sorry, Hank. It's very different from two-for-one cocktail hours, where a person of either sex can buy a cocktail at the same price. Ladies' nights set a double standard based on sex and that's sex discrimination, pure and simple.

HENRIETTA: So now you're a great foe of discrimination. How come you're not complaining that men haven't got an equal opportunity to participate half-naked in mud-wrestling contests? And why aren't you protesting the fact that women are paid less for doing the same jobs men do? You're a phony, Burt, and you make me sick.

BURT: Name calling is not a sign of a strong intellect. And why you should get so emotional over some lawyer's protest, I can't imagine. I guess it goes to show that women are more emotional than men.

3 ______________________________

LENA: I just found out that Sarah has been talking behind my back. That really brings me down, believe me. I've been a good friend to her, have gone out of my way to build her up and be there when she needed help. And now she betrays me.

CORA: The problem is your view of yourself. You put other people before yourself, so you set yourself up to be hurt. You have to learn to think of yourself first—to look out for number one.

LENA: That goes against everything I've been brought up to believe. My parents taught me that self-love is a sin and that thinking of others, caring for others, is the right way to live. It always made sense to me, too. The world certainly would be a better place if people were less selfish. But maybe you're right. Maybe I should protect my own interests and let other people take care of themselves.

CORA: If you'd done that with Sarah, you wouldn't be hurting so much now. Look at it this way—people who put others before themselves are either fools or masochists.

4 ______________________________

MAVIS: Big-time college varsity athletics is corrupt. Athletic departments entice high school athletes with false promises. They tell them they'll get a good education and then they enroll them in a smorgasbord of courses that don't lead to a degree. In many cases, they overlook the fact that the athletes don't have the basic academic skills to pass even the easiest courses.

CLINT: I don't know whether the situation is quite as bad as you make it out to be. But I admit it's not good. The majority of athletes in some sports never graduate. Still, I don't see what can be done to solve the problem.

MAVIS: There's no single solution. But I know several things that would be a good start to solving the problem. First, no student should be eligible for varsity athletics unless he or she is fully matriculated in a regular college program. And "individualized studies" programs shouldn't count as regular programs. Second, no student should be eligible unless he or she has completed one year of college. Third, every athlete should be required to maintain a C average.

CLINT: Sounds extreme to me. If those ideas were put into practice, it would mean the end of big-time college athletics. And that would deprive the fans of their pleasure, the colleges of substantial income, and the athletes of a chance to prepare for a professional career.

5 ______________________________

Note: A 200-pound fifteen-year-old boy was charged with torturing a two-year-old baby to death. While he was babysitting for the infant, the boy allegedly gave her alternately hot and cold showers and rammed her head against the wall because he enjoyed hearing her cry.[4]

MARVIN: I've never heard anything more disgusting than that. They shouldn't just execute the SOB, they should torture him the same way he tortured that little child.

JEREMY: I'm as outraged as you are, but if the law did that, then it would be acting on his level. And if we condoned such vengeance, we would be every bit as savage as he was. Moreso, perhaps, because we're sane and he was probably insane.

MARVIN: That's one of the problems in our criminal justice system. Every time people do something unbelievably creepy, we say they must have been insane. Why does he have to have been insane? How do you know that he wasn't just malicious?

JEREMY: Because no sane person would do such a sick thing. It's an abnormal act, and that proves the boy had an abnormal mind. Besides, what good would it do for society to take out its vengeance on him?

MARVIN: I'll tell you what good it would do. It would warn every other creep to think twice before even considering such a disgusting act. And equally important, it would balance the scales of justice.

6 ______________________________

Note: A 1982 U.S. Supreme Court ruling requires that states provide free public education to children of illegal aliens. The Census Bureau estimates that there are between one and six million illegal aliens in the United States. Others say ten million is a more accurate estimate.[5]

AGNES: What a ridiculous ruling. In effect, it rewards lawbreakers.

BELLE: What do you mean?

AGNES: Illegal aliens are lawbreakers: They enter the country without permission. If the states have to provide their children with free education, that means the taxpayers, U.S. citizens, are being made to provide benefits for people who have no right to them.

BELLE: Sure, it seems that way, but think of the other side of it. Rightly or wrongly, those people are living in this country, and it's in the interests of society to educate the children so they can become good citizens. Anyway, the children are not responsible for their parents' illegal acts. They are innocent victims and the state should regard them no differently from the children of citizens.

7 ______________________________

Note: A former Florida policewoman filed a federal discrimination suit, alleging that he was fired because of a scheduled sex-change operation. The officer, now a man, charged that the firing violated his constitutional rights and asked both monetary damages and reinstatement on the police force.[6]

CHRISTINE: If the cause for the firing was as the officer describes it, then it was improper.

RENEE: I disagree. A police officer is a public official and should not engage in behavior that disgraces that office.

CHRISTINE: What's disgraceful about having a sex-change operation?

RENEE: It's sick, strange, abnormal, and it makes the police department the laughingstock of the community.

CHRISTINE: Wrong. The only concern of the police department and of the general public should be the officer's performance of his or her duty. Whether he or she decides to have a sex-change operation is no more their business than if the officer decides to take up stamp collecting as a hobby.

8 ______________________________

IGNATIUS: It's sad that kids today don't have the kinds of heroes people had years ago, say back in the 1930s and 1940s.

FRANCIS: Having heroes just keeps a person from becoming an individual. Kids are better off when they try to be themselves, rather than imitating others.

IGNATIUS: I don't think so. It's impossible to live in society without role models of some kind. We pattern ourselves after our parents at first, and then we transfer our focus to someone else we look up to and admire. It's a very natural process and a healthy one as long as the people we admire are really admirable. The problem is that today many of them are not worthy of admiration.

FRANCIS: If I have children, I'll teach them not to imitate me or anyone, but to think their own thoughts and choose their own actions regardless of how others think and act. That way I can be sure they'll never be conformists.

9 ______________________________

Note: When an NBC engineer requested a paternity leave to help his wife care for their new baby, his request was denied. He decided to fight that decision in court, arguing that if women are eligible for six months of maternity leave with job and seniority guarantees, men should be eligible for similar paternity leaves.[7]

REGGIE: NBC was right in denying his request. A mother's situation is altogether different from a father's. To begin with, she undergoes all the physical strain of pregnancy and delivery and needs a period of recuperation. The father doesn't. Then, too, the degree of care she provides for the baby is in most cases greater than that provided by the father.

ALAN: Granted, the father doesn't experience pregnancy and delivery. But whether he or his wife will provide the greater degree of care for the infant can only be decided by the couple themselves. If the company provides such leaves for women, it should in fairness provide them for men, as well.

10 ________________________________

Note: According to legal tradition in the United States, there must be a dead body before a suspect can be charged with murder. The highest court in New York State broke that tradition in 1982 in deciding that a defendant's confession, coupled with circumstantial evidence, was sufficient basis for a murder trial, despite the fact that the body of the supposed murder victim was never found.[8]

KAREN: That decision will open the door to the miscarriage of justice.

HANNA: In what way?

KAREN: Because of that decision, mentally unstable people may falsely incriminate themselves and be tried for crimes that never occurred. For example, persons with guilt complexes may claim to have murdered someone they have found out is missing. The person may not be dead at all, but merely living somewhere else, in hiding from a wife or husband or from creditors.

HANNA: Such a situation is too farfetched to occur. In any case, the law shouldn't be based on such unlikely scenarios. The court's decision is a sound one.

11 ________________________________

QUENTIN: There'd be a lot less ignorance in the world today if parents didn't pass on their views to their children.

LOIS: How can they avoid doing so?

QUENTIN: By letting children form their own views. There's no law that says Democrats have to make little Democrats of their children, or that Protestants have to pass on their Protestantism.

LOIS: What should they do when their children ask them about politics or religion or democracy?

QUENTIN: Send them to the encyclopedia, or, if the parents are capable of objective explanation, explain to them the various views that are possible and encourage them to choose their own.

LOIS: How can you ask a three-year-old to make a choice about religion or politics or philosophy?

QUENTIN: In the case of young children the parents would simply explain as much as the children could understand and say that when they get older they can decide for themselves.

LOIS: How would all this benefit children or society?

QUENTIN: It would make it possible for children to grow up without their parents' prejudices and would help control the number of ignoramuses in the world.

12 ______________________________

Note: In 1983 a mentally unstable man called an Alabama television newsroom and threatened to kill himself. The station notified the police and then dispatched a camera crew to the scene. The crew reportedly stood by, filming, while the man doused himself with lighter fluid and lit two matches in an unsuccessful attempt to ignite himself. They only moved in to stop him after his third, successful attempt. The television station subsequently ran the film footage on the air. One member of the crew explained later, "My job is to record events as they happen."[9]

EDNA: The camera crew never should have let him light the first match. They should have stepped in immediately and restrained him until the police arrived.

LEON: But that wasn't their responsibility. Their responsibility was to obtain film for the news.

EDNA: That's insane. A human life was at stake. That's surely more important than the news. And what justification is there for the television station to air the tape? They should have had the decency to keep it off the news.

LEON: I don't think they had any such obligation either. The attempted suicide was news and their job is to report the news. True, it was grizzly, but the news often is. Your argument seems to be that everyone is his brother's keeper. I don't accept that view. If a nutty guy wants to set himself on fire, that's sad and even tragic. But that doesn't create any obligation for anyone else to prevent his doing so.

3 Making Important Distinctions

FREDA: My psychology professor said in class yesterday that people who are outwardly very happy, always laughing and joking, the life of the party, are often inwardly unhappy.

HORACE: You know, Eva is very much that way. I don't think I've ever seen her wearing a frown or having a negative word to say.

FREDA: There must be a terrible sadness she's hiding from everyone.

THE ERROR in reasoning in this dialogue is rather obvious. Freda leaps to a conclusion about Eva that the facts do not support. Less obvious, however, is the cause of Freda's error. It is her failure to distinguish between *often* and *always*. Her professor did not say that outwardly happy people are always inwardly unhappy, but that they often are. Therefore the description he gave the class may or may not apply to Eva, and it is incorrect to assume that it necessarily applies.

Distinctions are subtle differences between things, differences revealed by careful observation or analysis. Making important distinctions is a prerequisite of critical thinking.

WHY DISTINCTIONS ARE IMPORTANT

Whenever we read a dialogue or listen to a conversation, we are confronted with a host of similarities. The people involved speak the same language and use many of the same sentence patterns and words. In the case of complex issues, they may even present arguments that are in some respects very much alike. It is therefore easy for us to be confused, to experience difficulty noting the differences in what is being said. With our understanding thus blurred, it is impossible to analyze a dialogue effectively.

Sensitivity to distinctions enables us to get beyond the similarities and perceive the differences between arguments, even the subtle ones found in exchanges between informed dialoguers. Moreover, sensitivity to distinctions guides our thinking, helping us decide when to judge and when to withhold judgment, and which judgment is most appropriate. It spares us from such gross blunders as Freda's.

SEVEN CRUCIAL DISTINCTIONS

It would be impossible to list all the distinctions that are important to make in reading dialogues. They are simply too numerous, and in many cases their form changes as the particular situation changes. (For example, the distinction between *seldom* and *never* is essentially the same kind as that between *often* and *always,* yet the form is different.) Nevertheless, it is possible to identify the most crucial distinctions: those that must be made in virtually every critical thinking situation. The following seven distinctions are that kind.

The Distinction Between the Person and the Idea

The error of confusing the person and the idea is a common one. Advertisers use it to their advantage when they employ celebrities to promote their products. They know that many people will accept the product message uncritically because of their respect for the celebrity. Critical thinking demands that we judge ideas on their own merit, regardless of our feelings about the person who expresses them. You may, for example, believe Richard Nixon was a scoundrel who disgraced the office of the presidency, but if you are in the position of evaluating an idea advanced by Richard Nixon, you must set aside those feelings and give the idea a fair hearing. Similarly, if you admire Billy Graham, you must not allow that sentiment to become the basis for accepting his ideas uncritically.

To make the distinction between the person and the idea in your thinking, be alert to the temptation to dismiss or accept someone's words because of who that person is. When that temptation occurs, resist it.

The Distinction Between Preference and Judgment

Many people today consider every opinion about issues a matter of preference. "Everyone has a right to his or her opinion," they reason, "so whatever a person regards as reasonable is reasonable for that person and should not be challenged." Such thinking is muddled. It ignores the distinction between preference, which does not need to be defended, and judgment, which does. You may, for example, prefer red and green in combination, enjoy reading comic books more than traditional literature, and find the taste of squid appealing. However bizarre your taste in these matters may be in comparison with the standards of our culture, you need not apologize for them because there is no objective measure of taste. There is, however, an objective measure of judgment: how well it fits the facts.

How can you tell whether an assertion in a dialogue (or an assertion of your own) should be considered an expression of preference or judgment? Ask whether the assertion essentially says, "I like this" or "I like this better than that," as expressions of preference do, or whether it says "This is so" or "This ought to be believed (or done)," as expressions of judgment do. Examples of judgment are "The Social Security system is in trouble," "Capital punishment should be reinstated," "God exists," and, as we saw in the opening dialogue of this chapter, "There must be a terrible sadness [Eva's] hiding from everyone." If the assertion is a judgment, then it must be evaluated in light of the evidence that supports or challenges it.

The Distinction Between Relevant and Irrelevant Material

Unlike written communication, conversation seldom moves in a straight line. People say what comes to mind, and thoughts do not always occur in logical, organized fashion. So dialoguers may begin discussing one issue and then abruptly and unconsciously turn to a second issue and perhaps a third. The longer the dialogue continues, the greater the number of issues it is likely to contain. The result is that many dialogues contain a number of ideas that are largely irrelevant to one or more of the issues discussed. Effective analysis depends upon separating relevant from irrelevant points.

To make the distinction between relevant and irrelevant material, identify the issue(s) as soon as possible in your reading of the dialogue. Then decide in what way, if any, each point made in the dialogue is related to the issue(s).

The Distinction Between More Important and Less Important Points

Just as not everything that is stated in a dialogue is necessarily relevant to the issue(s), not everything that is relevant is of equal importance. Statements made in conversation are like gems: They differ significantly in quality. Some are of great value, others are worthless, and most fall somewhere between the two extremes. Moreover many of the most glittering, which seem to be precious, are in reality worth very little.

To compound the problem, there are no easy ways to identify the most important points. They are not necessarily prominently placed, occurring sometimes in offhand remarks whose significance is missed even by the people who make them. On occasion, the most important points about an issue will not be expressed at all. (On those occasions, it will be up to you to identify and express them in your analysis of the issue.)

The value of the distinction between more important and less important points in dialogue is that it helps us assess arguments on something more trustworthy than general impressions. If we fail to make this distinction, we will be tempted to confuse quantity with quality and judge an argument on the basis of how much evidence is presented for it. The distinction reminds us that quality is at least as important as quantity, that one compelling item of evidence can outweigh a half-dozen lesser items.

To be sure you do not overlook the distinction between more important and less important points, consider the relative merits of both the points made by the dialoguers and the points you recognized were omitted and added yourself.

The Distinction Between Form and Substance

The form of people's expression can affect us independently of the substance of that expression. Eloquence is an especially powerful factor. A person with the gift of words can sometimes so impress us that we fail to note the weaknesses in his or her argument. Well-chosen phrases can capture the imagination and make us endorse false or shallow assessments of situations and unrealistic approaches to problems. This danger is especially great in those dialogues where one speaker has a markedly greater command of language than the other.

To distinguish between form and substance, after your initial reading of the dialogue ask yourself whether one speaker is more skilled with words than the other. Whenever you find that to be the case, make a special effort to judge the quality of the ideas apart from the skill with which they are expressed.

The Distinction Between Assertion and Evidence

Asserting is saying that something is so or ought to be believed or done. Providing evidence is substantiating that something is so or ought to be believed or done. The human mind can not only produce conclusions; it can do so with or without evidence. In fact, some people are in the habit of piling assertion upon assertion, never bothering to substantiate what they say. What makes matters worse is that to the unobservant a string of assertions without supporting evidence is indistinguishable from adequately supported assertions.

Critical thinking demands that we distinguish not only between supported and unsupported assertions, but also between well-supported and poorly supported assertions, and even, in more refined dialogues, between well-supported and better-supported assertions. The key to making these distinctions lies in consciously separating assertions from evidence. If you are not accustomed to doing this, you can acquire the habit by taking an extra step in your analysis of each dialogue in this chapter: Mark every assertion with one color magic marker and every supporting statement with a different color.

The Distinction Between Familiarity and Validity

We are naturally more comfortable with familiar things than with unfamiliar. Like watchdogs, we tend to bark loudest at the new and unexpected. At times this tendency is so strong that familiar ideas in dialogues will seem more reasonable than unfamiliar ones. And if we do not check this tendency, it can lead us to endorse inferior views. To be sure you observe this distinction, remind yourself from time to time that every creative development, every breakthrough in understanding, every ingenious solution to life's problems first appears as a new idea. In addition, if you tend to be trustful of the old and distrustful of the new, make a conscious effort to give unfamiliar ideas a fair hearing.

MAINTAINING OBJECTIVITY

Your success in making important distinctions when you read a dialogue will depend on one additional consideration: your ability to examine arguments objectively. Examining objectively means setting aside personal feelings, desires, and special interests and focusing on the evidence. Though this may sound easy to do, it is seldom so. One of the main obstacles to objectivity is the fact that most of us tend to assume that we already possess it and therefore needn't bother to strive for it. In reality objectivity is not the kind of quality that remains ours once we gain it; it is a fleeting quality that is lost the moment we relax our efforts to maintain it.

The basic approach to maintaining your objectivity may be summed up in one brief rule: Always understand before evaluating, and evaluate before deciding. If you follow this rule scrupulously, you will avoid the trap many people fall into, the trap of approaching a dialogue wanting one side to be correct and then unconsciously bending their interpretation of evidence so that they can go on believing as they wish.

WRITING TIP: CLARIFY YOUR DISTINCTIONS

Many writers assume that the mere mention of a distinction will be sufficient for their readers to understand it and appreciate its significance. That assumption is unwarranted. What is clear to one person is not necessarily clear to others, and few ideas are so simple that they cannot be misunderstood. This is especially true of issues about which people strongly disagree. Responsible writers take care to explain their distinctions fully.

To be sure you handle distinctions effectively in your compositions, adopt this guideline: *Whenever you are calling your readers' attention to an important distinction, don't just state its importance; rather, explain fully enough to eliminate any confusion that might exist.* Here, for example, is the way you might present the distinction between *often* and *always* that Freda failed to make in the dialogue that opened this chapter:

> **There's a big difference between *often* and *always*. Freda's professor said that people who are outwardly very happy are OFTEN inwardly unhappy. He was talking about many cases, not ALL cases. Eva's case may fit his description, but then again it may not. There's no way of deciding without more evidence than we have. Therefore it's wrong to conclude that Eva is inwardly unhappy. The most that we can say is that she *may* be.**

The need for adequate explanation, of course, is not limited to situations in which you are making distinctions. It is present in any situation in which your readers might misunderstand your statements or their relevance to the issue you are discussing. Though it would be impossible in this brief space to list all such situations, here are the most important ones.

1. Whenever you are stating your choice of one idea over alternative ideas, explain your reasons for that choice.
2. Whenever you are arguing that certain evidence is more compelling than other evidence, explain why it is more compelling.
3. Whenever you are defining terms, explain how the terms differ from similar terms or how your special use of the terms differs from common use.

4. Whenever you are mentioning causes and effects and there is any chance that your readers will be uncertain of the relationship between them, explain the process by which the effects occur.

To realize just how important thorough explanations are to the effectiveness of your writing, reflect for a moment on how you usually react when you pick up a magazine and begin reading an article and then find that the writer never bothered to explain her ideas clearly, but instead left you to struggle with her meaning. Chances are you toss the magazine aside and say to yourself, "If this writer couldn't be bothered to make her meaning clear, I'm not going to waste my time reading her article." That is precisely how others will respond to your writing if it lacks clear explanations.

SAMPLE COMPOSITION

Here is a sample composition together with the dialogue that prompted it, demonstrating how to make distinctions clearly.

The Dialogue

In 1982 a group of Sioux Indians set up a camp in the Black Hills of South Dakota, claiming that they had a legal right to be there because the place was a holy land to their ancestors and remains important in the practice of the Sioux religion, which teaches that the Lakota Sioux emerged from the underground spirit world into the Black Hills millions of years ago. The Sioux want the area turned into a permanent religion-based community. The U.S. Forest Service, which owns the land, wants them evicted.[1]

QUINELLA: The courts should decide in favor of the Indians. The land belonged to them originally.

RONNIE: Forget about the situation centuries ago. Today the land belongs to the U.S. Forest Service. They hold it in trust for all Americans. It can't just be given away to a group of people because their ancestors lived there.

QUINELLA: It's not just a case of their ancestors having lived there. It was and still is their holy land, a sacred place. The situation is very much like the situation with Israel. The land not only belonged to their ancestors but continues to have religious significance to them.

RONNIE: Don't compare the Sioux religion with Judaism. Belief in a journey from an underground spirit world is primitive!

The Composition

A Place to Pray

Imagine the impact on the world if the American Indians' claims to the land they once roamed were honored. Centuries of carefully recorded land transactions would be discarded and millions of people in the United States and Canada would be uprooted and sent to Europe, Asia, and Africa, continents they had never even visited. And when they arrived there they would have no recourse but to search long-forgotten history to find and press ancient claims of their own. The global disruption that would follow such an event would be unparalleled.

What would the impact be? Instead of leaving the readers to guess, the author devotes the rest of the paragraph to explaining.

It is wise that there is an unwritten statute of limitations in such matters. That is not to say that the Indians' claim is not legitimate. Though our history books say that European explorers "discovered" America, that is inaccurate. It is improper to speak of discovery when people already inhabit the land. If it were proper, then some hardy band of weekend boaters might "discover" New Orleans or Staten Island and expect the residents to pack up their belongings and leave.

Here the author clarifies the distinction between what is believed to take place in the act of "discovery" and what actually takes place.

However, the fact that the government must disallow Indian claims in general does not mean that it should never honor a particular claim. From time to time a claim may arise that has sufficient merit for the government to make at least a token nod to justice and acknowledge the historic injury to the Indians. I believe the Sioux claim to the Black Hills has such merit.

To begin with, the land is owned by the federal government rather than by individuals, so no one would be denied rights he or she acquired in good faith. Nor would the people of the United States, in whose trust the government holds the land, suffer any great financial loss. After all, the Department of the Interior in recent years has sold hundreds of thousands of acres of federal land at what many experts say are bargain prices.

The final three paragraphs of the composition explain the factors that distinguish the Sioux claim to the Black Hills holy land from most other Indian land claims.

Even more important than the relative inexpensiveness of honoring the claim is the nature of the claim. The Sioux want the land because it is a holy land to them, the place from which the Lakota Sioux emerged from the underground spirit world millions of years ago. Many people undoubtedly have little sympathy for Indian religion, which they regard as primitive and therefore of less value than the "higher" religions. But no one who understands the historic importance of religious freedom, the same freedom that brought most Americans' ancestors to this land, will deny the importance of overcoming such feelings and regarding Indian religion with tolerance and respect.

Giving the Sioux a small part of the vast wilderness we own, a place for them to pray, will cost us little. Yet the symbolic value of that gift will be great. We owe it to ourselves, as much as to them, to do so.

DIALOGUE EXERCISES

Analyze each of the following dialogues, being especially careful to note important distinctions. Then write a composition on one of the dialogues, presenting and supporting your view and applying the writing tip given at the end of the chapter.

1 ______________________________

Note: A ten-year-old New Jersey boy filed a $180,000 lawsuit against his twelve-year-old sister after she threw a pencil at him and caused extensive injuries to his eye. The lawsuit would enable the family to recover medical expenses under a homeowner's insurance policy.[2]

GUS: The court should throw that lawsuit out. There's no precedent for it. It's just a gimmick to collect on the insurance.

STAN: It's an ingenious approach, all right, but not a gimmick.

GUS: You're splitting hairs. How can a kid sue his own sister? They're members of the same family. Where were the parents anyway? If they let something like that happen, they deserve to foot the medical bills.

STAN: That's unreasonable. Did your parents watch you every minute of every day? No matter how responsible parents are, accidents happen, although in this case it was not really an accident.

GUS: What do you mean it wasn't an accident?

STAN: She threw it at him in anger. That constitutes the desire to do harm, which is the definition of malice. And since it was a malicious act, the lawsuit makes perfect sense.

GUS: But she's his sister. Whoever heard of suing your sister for such a thing?

2 ______________________________

Note: The U.S. Supreme Court has ruled that a driver's refusal to take a blood-alcohol test can be used as evidence against him or her.[3]

MONICA: Now that's a sensible court decision.

AIDAN: I disagree.

MONICA: How can you possibly disagree? The only conceivable reason a person would refuse to take such a test would be that he's drunk and fears losing his license.

AIDAN: Not at all. He many refuse because he's convinced that the state has no right to make a person incriminate himself.

MONICA: I can't believe you. How by any stretch of the imagination does a blood-alcohol test make a person incriminate herself? And notice, please, that I changed your chauvinistic *HIMself* to *HERself*.

AIDAN: Your word is no less chauvinistic than mine. And it's obvious how he incriminates himself by taking a blood-alcohol test: He provides the police with evidence that can convict him of a crime.

MONICA: Ahah! You just admitted that he'd be convicted. That proves my point. It only works against someone who's drunk. Sober people needn't worry.

AIDAN: It's pointless to argue with you. You can't stick to the issue.

3 ______________________________

OLAF: Did you know that poisonous snake handling is a legal religious ritual in only one state in the Union, West Virginia?

WINNIE: That's one state too many.

OLAF: Why do you say that? People don't handle the snakes capriciously. They do it out of religious conviction.

WINNIE: What kind of nutty religion would advocate such a thing?

OLAF: Would you believe Christianity? It says in Mark 16:17–18, "And these signs will accompany those who have believed: in My name they will cast out demons, they will speak with new tongues; they will pick up serpents, and if they drink any deadly poison, it shall not hurt them. . . ."

WINNIE: I'm not sure I believe you. I'm going to check it out in my *Bible*. But even if it says that, I still think it's nutty.

OLAF: Careful, Winnie, that's getting very close to blasphemy.

WINNIE: Well, that's what I think. I can't imagine any reason such a deadly game should be legalized.

OLAF: I'll give you one—because the state has no right to restrict religious practices. Separation of church and state cuts both ways. We're always so concerned about some religion's taking control of the state. Well, it can work in reverse too. The state can gain control of religion, and that's just as big a wrong. Any practice done in the name of religion should be legal.

4 ______________________________

Note: A U.S. Circuit Court judge upheld a Monroe County, Michigan, hospital's policy of admitting in the delivery room only members of the mother's immediate family. The policy had been challenged by an unmarried man who had been denied admission to the delivery of his child.[4]

VIC: What a shame. Here was a man who wanted to be present for one of the most beautiful moments in life, as an expression of love, and a stupid judge prevented him from being there.

PRISCILLA: How do you know it was an act of love? Maybe it was morbid curiosity that motivated him. And if he was so big on expressions of love, why didn't he marry the woman?

VIC: Believe it or not, you can love someone without marrying her. Maybe he was already married and some legal obstacle prevented him from getting a divorce. Maybe he wanted to be married, but the woman preferred to live together. Not every woman wants to get married, you know.

PRISCILLA: The hospital is not the villain, as you imply. They have a perfect right to set such a policy. Our society still frowns on unmarried people having children.

VIC: What business does society have running people's lives?

PRISCILLA: They're not running people's lives. They're standing up for morality.

5 ________________________________

NANCY: All the newspapers and magazines seem to be running articles on what's wrong with the nation's schools. But they're overlooking the biggest problem.

INEZ: What's that?

NANCY: The fact that patriotism isn't taught any more.

INEZ: How can patriotism be taught?

NANCY: In lots of ways. By reciting the pledge of allegiance to the flag and singing patriotic songs, for example.

INEZ: Sounds kind of hokey to me. I don't see how that stuff would teach patriotism anyway.

NANCY: Those were just examples. Teachers could also introduce discussions of the principles our country was founded on and how they differ from those of undemocratic countries. They could have students appreciate what makes our country special.

INEZ: That kind of teaching is little more than brainwashing. Waving the flag, "My country right or wrong," all that jerky stuff, doesn't make people appreciate their country more—it just makes them want to join the army and start wars.

6 ________________________________

Note: The Georgia Supreme Court ruled that a church founded by a woman who considers herself "a pagan and a witch" is entitled to a property tax exemption on the building it uses for worship.[5]

DIANE: Now I've heard everything. How can people in their right minds confuse superstition with religion that way?

TINA: I agree with you. Witchcraft is the exact opposite of religion. It's like confusing capitalism and communism. Ridiculous.

DIANE: Can you imagine the services they hold there? They probably run around naked, stick pins in dolls, and howl at the moon.

TINA: Don't laugh. They really do that kind of stuff. A lot of their so-called worship is sexual: perverted things. They call it religion to ease the guilt feelings they have about their perversion. What's that term we learned in psychology last semester?

DIANE: *Rationalization?*

TINA: Right.

7 ____________________

Note: A man was walking his dog along the ocean shore during a gale when the dog was swept into the sea by a wave. The man plunged in after him. Seeing the man struggling, five police officers attempted to save him. The man and three of the officers perished.[6]

JOE: What a touching story. A man losing his life in an attempt to save an animal. With all the selfishness in today's world, it's refreshing to learn that some people still care for something besides themselves.

VINCE: That's not the meaning I find in it. To me it's a story of stupidity. A man not only throwing his own life away for a worthless animal, but also causing the police officers to lose their lives.

JOE: He didn't cause them to die. They didn't have to jump in after him. They chose to, and I think it speaks well of them that they did.

VINCE: You're missing the point. He put them on the spot. They are trained to respond to human need. They really had no free choice in the matter. So he killed them . . . and all because he didn't have the sense to use his God-given brain.

JOE: That's right, make a hero out to be a chump. People like you are the reason there's so much pessimism in the world.

8 ____________________

TERESA: With all the alcohol-related accidents among young drivers, I wish they'd raise the drinking age to twenty-five.

FRITZ: That's easy for you to say because you're already twenty-five. You'd think differently if you were twenty-two or twenty-three.

TERESA: I don't think so. I believe such a move would save many lives. That's my reason for advocating it, not because I'm twenty-five.

FRITZ: Well, I'm against it. I waited and waited to be able to drink legally. And now that I can, I surely wouldn't stand quietly by for such an unfair change. Where'd you ever get such an idea anyway?

TERESA: I didn't just make it up. I heard Senator Worthy explaining why he favors the idea, and he made a lot of sense.

FRITZ: I should have known there'd be a politician behind a crazy idea. He's the same one who supports gun control. Did you ever get a good look at the guy? He's got shifty eyes. I wouldn't support anything he favored.

9 ______________________________

Note: A Colorado judge sentenced a thirteen-year-old boy to thirty days in the county jail after the youth had been convicted of his third motor vehicle offense within three years. The final offense involved taking the family car, backing down a hill, crossing a lane of traffic on a busy road, and ramming into a ditch.[7]

MIKE: Do you agree with what the judge did?

GAIL: Of course. What choice did he have? The boy obviously didn't have any respect for the rights of others, other motorists and pedestrians, for example, and his parents undoubtedly couldn't control him. Otherwise he'd have learned his lesson the first or second time.

MIKE: I don't know. I can see your point. But somehow it seems wrong to put a young kid in jail. It brands him a criminal and he might not be able to live that label down. It also suggests there's no hope for him, that society is giving up on him.

GAIL: That's silly. It's just another way of dealing with the boy's problem. A more serious way, to be sure. But if other methods have failed, I can't see any alternative.

MIKE: Maybe they could fine the parents. He's their child so they should be responsible for what he does.

10 ______________________________

MAUREEN: Should a woman who has lived with a man for a number of years without being married be granted alimony when they break up?

LESTER: They call that "palimony" in such cases. And the answer to your question is a resounding no.

MAUREEN: Why not?

LESTER: Simple. Because they're not married: no contract, no obligation.

MAUREEN: Come on. You can surely have a contract without a formal ceremony or a piece of paper signed by both parties. Isn't the fact of their living together a clear indication of an unwritten agreement?

LESTER: Of course, it signifies an agreement, an agreement to go on living together as long as both want to. But only that long, and with no strings attached.

MAUREEN: What if the woman supports him—for example, while he's in graduate school? Doesn't she have a right to palimony in that case?

LESTER: If she supports him without a written agreement to protect herself, then she's a jerk. And the law should not be required to offer protection for her lack of judgment.

11 ________________________________

Note: When an unmarried high school biology teacher in a Long Island, New York, school became pregnant, a group of parents petitioned the school board to fire her. They reasoned that her pregnancy was proof of immorality and that allowing her to remain a teacher would set a poor example for students. The school board refused to fire her.[8]

AUTHUR: Good for the school board. Their action must have taken courage. Pious hypocrites can generate a lot of pressure.

GUINEVERE: Why do you call them hypocrites? They had a right to express their view.

ARTHUR: Do you mean you agree with that nonsense about the pregnant teacher's being immoral and a poor example to students?

GUINEVERE: Yes, I suppose I do. Not that I think everybody deserves firing from her job in such circumstances. I think teachers are in a special category. More should be expected of them. They should have to measure up to a higher standard of conduct than people in other occupations because they are in charge of young people's education, and young people are impressionable.

4 Recognizing Errors in Reasoning

GERTRUDE: English is a chauvinistic language. And one of the worst offenses is using the male pronoun to refer to people in general. Even professors do it. They say "Everybody hand in *his* paper now." "Someone left *his* pen in my office yesterday." It infuriates me.

HEATHCLIFF: Professor Lindquist says that's not a chauvinistic practice; it's a simple matter of agreement, the singular *he* following the singular *everybody* or *someone*. And he ought to know; he's a linguist.

GERTRUDE: He's also a man . . . and that disqualifies him from commenting on chauvinism.

HEATHCLIFF: Besides, that use of *he* has been standard for centuries. It's a tradition of our language and shouldn't be violated.

THIS BRIEF dialogue between Gertrude and Heathcliff contains several errors in reasoning. That is not surprising. Few exchanges of viewpoint between people are error-free. This is often due to the tendency of many people to form and express their opinions too uncritically. Such people seldom think; rather, they behave without thinking. In other words, they express the view impulse dictates or the one they have heard expressed so often by others that it seems indisputable.

Errors, of course, do not befall only uncritical people. As we have seen in previous chapters, even the most meticulous efforts to be reasonable can be upset. We can omit important considerations, misinterpret or incorrectly evaluate evidence, and draw conclusions that do not fit the evidence. In addition, we can perceive selectively, pretend to know, favor familiar views, practice face-saving, and overlook important distinctions.

LOOKING FOR ERRORS

Recognizing errors in dialogues would be easy to do if every error were clearly labeled. That, however, is not the case. The fact that a line of thought is flawed or that a conclusion does not fit the evidence that is presented is not always readily discernible. To the uncritical eye all statements in a dialogue can look confusingly alike.

To develop skill in recognizing errors you must first maintain your awareness that errors are likely to be present. That means checking your tendency to slip into an uncritical frame of mind and accept what is said as being correct merely because someone says it. To find errors you must be ready to see them. So whenever you read a dialogue, say to yourself, "Even if the participants in this dialogue are trying to reason well, they are likely to slip from time to time. I will be alert for those slips." Second, to recognize errors you must know what to look for: to understand when and where errors are most likely to occur, to know the telltale signs of the most common errors, and to be able to distinguish them from valid reasoning.

COMMON ERRORS IN DIALOGUES

The ten reasoning errors we will discuss in this chapter are not the only ones you will find in dialogues, but they are the most common ones. By becoming familiar with them you will be able to identify where most arguments go wrong and determine how to set them right again.

Either-Or Thinking

The error in either-or thinking consists of viewing a particular reality solely in terms of opposing extremes when, in fact, other views are possible. It is often accompanied by the demand that people choose between the two extremes and the clear, if often unstated, suggestion that no third choice is possible. Here is an example of either-or thinking:

GERTRUDE: The real aim of religion is perfecting one's self. Nothing else but that matters.

HEATHCLIFF: That's not true. The real aim is loving one's neighbor. If your focus is on yourself, you simply aren't a religious person.

Now it may be that one or the other of these aims is the "real" aim of religion. But it may also be that religion has two or three or eighteen important aims. To discount that possibility even before considering it is unreasonable. Whenever you encounter either-or thinking, ask, "Why must it be one or the other? Why not both (or neither)?"

Stereotyping

Stereotyping is ignoring someone's or something's individuality and focusing instead on some preconceived notion about the person or thing. (It is one of the central features of prejudice.) There are stereotyped notions about Jews and blacks and atheists and political parties—in short, about many things. Here is an example:

GERTRUDE: Are you going to that public lecture tonight, the one about the effects of exercise on stress? The local tennis coach is delivering it.

HEATHCLIFF: I wouldn't waste my time listening to some dumb jock's simple-minded muttering.

Is the coach an authority on the subject he is lecturing on? Has he done research? Has he written articles or books? These are reasonable matters to inquire about. But Heathcliff's negative stereotyping smothers his curiosity and makes fair judgment impossible. Whenever you encounter such prefabricated assessments of an entire class of people or things, ask, "What evidence is offered that the assessment fits the individual in question?"

Attacking the Person

Another error consists of disposing of an argument by attacking the person who advances it. It is not a reasonable approach because an argument's validity does not depend on the character of its advocates. A scoundrel may, on occasion, support a valid argument, and a saint an invalid one. Here is an example of attacking the person:

GERTRUDE: Arthur Dean is organizing a group to protest the tearing down of the Hastings Mansion. He believes its historic value is too great to let it be sacrificed for a shopping center. I'm going to join.

HEATHCLIFF: You're crazy to join. Dean is a real lowlife. He runs around with other girls behind his fiance's back and uses his roommate's things without permission. Besides, he sponges off everyone.

Everything Heathcliff says about Dean may be accurate. And yet it sheds no light on whether the protest Dean is organizing is worthy of support. Whenever you find an attack on a person in a dialogue, ask, "Are the charges being made against the person relevant to the issue under discussion?" If they are not, refuse to consider them in your analysis.

Contradiction

Contradiction occurs when a person makes two assertions that are logically inconsistent with each other. It is an error that occurs more often in long dialogues than in short ones and is more difficult to detect than other errors because the conflicting assertions seldom appear together. To detect contradiction you must remember each dialoguer's early assertions and recognize their relationship to later assertions. Here is an example of a contradiction in dialogue:

GERTRUDE: Morally, our nation is in big trouble. Let me give you an example. For centuries, the taking of a life was regarded as wrong. That's as it should be. No one is ever justified in taking a human life. Yet today books and articles are written defending so-called mercy killing and giving directions on how to commit suicide.

[Later in the dialogue, after several exchanges with Heathcliff, Gertrude speaks again.]

GERTRUDE: I still say we've grown too casual about human life. The only situation in which the taking of a life is ever justified is self-defense.

First Gertrude says the taking of a human life is never justified. Then she says there is a situation in which it is justified. That is a contradiction. Whenever you encounter a contradiction in a person's argument, ask, "Does the contradiction invalidate the person's entire argument or only a part of it? And if a part, which part?" A note of caution is in order here. Careful inspection of what at first glance appear to be contradictions will often reveal they are not contradictions at all. If, for example, Gertrude had said, "No one should ever be applauded for taking a human life," instead of "No one is ever justified in taking a human life," she could not fairly be charged with contradicting herself, at least until you knew what she meant by "applauded."

Faulty Analogy

Analogy is a line of reasoning suggesting that things alike in one respect are also alike in other respects. Analogy is a very common kind of reasoning and there is nothing wrong with it as long as the similarities that are claimed are real. An analogy is faulty when they are not real.

Here is an example of faulty analogy:

GERTRUDE: I hear the government is requiring that stronger warnings be placed on cigarette packages and in advertisements.

HEATHCLIFF: Putting warnings on cigarette packages is as foolish as putting "Warning! Eating too much of this product may make you a fat slob!" on packages of spaghetti or "Warning! Careless use of this instrument may smash your fingers" on hammers.

Heathcliff's analogies are vivid, but faulty. Eating spaghetti is good for people, if done in moderation; it provides nutrition. Smoking cigarettes does no comparable good. Similarly, the hammer can do harm if used carelessly. But cigarettes have been shown to do harm no matter how carefully they are used. Whenever you encounter any analogy, say, "Granted, these two things may be similar in certain respects, but are there any respects in which they are dissimilar?"

Faulty Causation

Faulty causation may take either of two forms. The first is concluding that one thing caused another merely because of their proximity in time or space. For example, shortly after a black cat crosses someone's path, an accident befalls her, so she concludes that the cat's crossing her path caused her misfortune. This error occurs not only in everyday reasoning, but in formal reasoning as well. For many years the prevailing medical opinion was that damp night air causes malaria simply because the onset of the disease occurred after exposure to night air. (The real cause, mosquitoes, which happened to be more active in evening hours, was discovered much later.)

The other form taken by faulty causation is concluding that learning why people are interested in an issue is the same as evaluating their thinking about the issue. "Find the motivation," goes this reasoning, "and you have determined whether that argument is valid." This line of reasoning, which resembles attacking the person, is erroneous for a similar reason. A person's motivation for advancing an argument is never sufficient reason for approving or rejecting an argument. Noble motives may underlie bad arguments and ignoble motives good ones. Here is an example of this form of faulty causation:

GERTRUDE: Professor McCready told my class today he believes the way student evaluations are used on this campus doesn't provide effective evaluations of the quality of teaching. He said the questions themselves are OK, but the evaluation should be made at the end of the semester instead of during the tenth week. He blasted the administration, saying they are more concerned with suiting their schedules than getting meaningful input from students. He made a lot of sense.

HEATHCLIFF: Sometimes you're really naive, Gertie. Didn't you even wonder why he attacked the testing procedure? If you had done so, you'd know. It must be he got scorched by students on the evaluation last semester. If he'd received a good rating, he'd be praising the evaluation process. So much for his "sensible argument."

Perhaps Heathcliff is correct in what he says about the professor. Perhaps he did get a poor evaluation last semester. And perhaps that's what prompted him to take a critical look at the evaluation procedure. So what? That would be a normal reaction, yet it has no bearing on the validity of his argument about student evaluation of teachers. That argument can be appraised only by examining the evidence that supports or challenges it.

Whenever you encounter an assertion that one thing has caused another, ask, "Is the proximity in time or space evidence of a true cause/effect relationship or merely a coincidence?" Whenever you find an argument being approved or rejected because of a person's motivation, remember that motivation is irrelevant and test the argument against the evidence.

Irrational Appeal

There are four common kinds of irrational appeal: appeals to emotion, to tradition or faith, to moderation, and to authority. Each of these is a misuse of a rational appeal and may be identified as follows:

An *appeal to emotion* is rational when it accompanies thought and analysis, and irrational when it substitutes for them.

An *appeal to tradition or faith* is rational when the particular practice or belief is regarded in light of present circumstances, and irrational when it means "Let's continue to do (believe) as we have done merely because we have always done so."

An *appeal to moderation* is rational when the moderate approach is offered as the best solution to the problem or issue, and irrational when moderation is merely a convenient way to avoid offending someone or to evade the responsibility of judging.

An *appeal to authority* is rational when it acknowledges the fallibility of people and their institutions and the possibility of differing interpretations, and irrational when it disallows reasonable questions and challenges. (As used here, *authority* means not only eminent people, but also eminent books and documents, such as the *Bible* and the U.S. Constitution, and eminent agencies, such as the Supreme Court.)

Here are some examples of irrational appeals:

GERTRUDE: I can't understand how any sensitive person can be opposed to the control of handguns.

HEATHCLIFF: To begin with, Americans have always been free to bear arms. It's a part of our heritage to do so if we wish. But if you need more proof than that, consider the Constitution. It specifically refers to the freedom to bear arms as a right of every citizen.

GERTRUDE: But the framers of the Constitution couldn't have envisioned the problems of modern society when they were writing. Therefore their meaning . . .

HEATHCLIFF: It's the responsibility of a loyal American to defend the Constitution, not to question it.

Both of Heathcliff's arguments are irrational. The first, that Americans should be free to bear arms because they have been free to do so in the past, is an irrational appeal to tradition. The second, that it is an act of disloyalty to question the Constitution, is an irrational appeal to authority.

Hasty Conclusion

A hasty conclusion is one that is drawn without appropriate evidence. In other words, it is a conclusion chosen without sufficient reason from two or more possible conclusions. Hasty conclusions are especially tempting in situations where prior opinions compromise objectivity. Those opinions make a person wish for a particular conclusion to be so, and wishing leads to uncritical acceptance. Here is an example of a hasty conclusion:

GERTRUDE: How did you make out with that part-time job you were applying for?

HEATHCLIFF: I didn't get it, and I know very well why too. It's because I'm not black or Hispanic and I'm not a woman.

GERTRUDE: How do you know that was the reason?

HEATHCLIFF: Come on, Gertie. You know perfectly well that minorities have an advantage in today's job market.

Even if Heathcliff were right about minorities' having an advantage in the job market (and considerable evidence challenges that view), his conclusion about his failure to get the job is hasty. The fact that something is generally true is not sufficient evidence that it is true in a particular case. It is possible that Heathcliff was passed over because of lack of experience or a bad attitude or some other reason. Whenever you encounter any conclusion, ask whether the evidence is sufficient to warrant choosing it over other possible conclusions.

Overgeneralization

A generalization is a judgment about a class of people or things made after observation of a number of members of that class. Overgeneralization is generalization based upon insufficient observation. One of the most common errors in argument, overgeneralization may be explained by the natural human tendency to classify sensory data tidily, and by the difficulty of determining what, in any given situation, constitutes "sufficient evidence." Accordingly, people are often found making careless assertions about whole groups of people and things. Here are some examples:

GERTRUDE: Ever since I arrived on campus last month, I've been appalled by the manners of the students here. They're unbelievably boorish.

HEATHCLIFF: Yes, and the townspeople are so unfriendly, too. I don't know why I ever picked this college.

GERTRUDE: Oh, I'm not sorry I came here. The professors are very helpful and encouraging. They go out of their way to explain things.

We don't know how many students are enrolled in the college, what the population of the town is, or how many professors are on the college staff. But however small the college and the town are, it is unlikely that Gertrude and Heathcliff have had enough contact with people to justify their level of generalization. Whenever you encounter a statement about entire groups of people or things, look for evidence that the observations have been sufficient in number and that the person has demonstrated that what was observed is typical of the group in general. If that evidence is lacking in the dialogue, and your own experience does not provide it, you may conclude that you are dealing with an overgeneralization.

Oversimplification

It is natural to want to simplify matters; simplification aids understanding and communication. For that reason, simplification is legitimate—as long as it does not distort the reality it describes. When it does that, it becomes oversimplification. The most frequent kind of oversimplification that occurs in dialogues is the presentation of only one side of a two-sided (or three- or four-sided) reality. Here is an example of such oversimplification:

GERTRUDE: I'm really looking forward to being a high school teacher some day. I only hope I can meet the demands of the profession.

HEATHCLIFF: Demands? High school teachers have it made. They're through at three o'clock every day and only work nine months of the year. The only cushier job I know of is the job of a college professor.

There is some truth in what Heathcliff says. The high school class schedule usually ends at 3:00 P.M. and the official work year, with holidays and summer vacation time considered, is nine months. But that is only part of the complex reality of high school teaching. Many teachers are responsible for five different classes each day, each of which requires preparation for lectures and discussions, and for the grading of homework. All that work must be done after 3:00 P.M. In addition, teachers are often expected to chaperone after-school activities and advise clubs and organizations. Finally, they are required to extend their knowledge of the subject matter they teach by pursuing graduate degrees in their spare time. To ignore all these duties is to oversimplify the reality of high school teaching.

There is no easy formula for detecting oversimplification. Your best approach is to be suspicious of any brief description of a complex reality. When you encounter one, ask, "Is it really this neat and simple? Is there another side to the reality that is not represented here?"

AVOIDING "FALLACY FRENZY"

Looking for errors can be an enjoyable activity, so enjoyable, in fact, that we may find ourselves in a state of "fallacy frenzy."[1] In that state we behave much like a school of sharks in a feeding frenzy, excited by weakness and vulnerability, and ripping and tearing at arguments indiscriminately. When we approach the job of finding errors in dialogues that way, we lose sight of our larger purpose: finding the truth about issues.

To avoid fallacy frenzy, remember to look for errors not merely for the sake of finding them, but as a step toward constructing the most reasonable view of the issue. Further, when you have finished examining a dialogue for errors, look back over both sides of the argument and decide what points are valid and therefore worth incorporating into your judgment. Finally, keep these principles in mind:

The presence of an error does not necessarily invalidate an argument. (Although errors always weaken an argument, not all errors are equally serious. And even the best argument may contain numerous errors when presented by a careless thinker.)

The absence of error is no guarantee that an argument is the best possible one. (It merely establishes the argument's candidacy for that distinction.)

WRITING TIP: CLARIFY LOGICAL RELATIONSHIPS

All good writing is coherent; that is, it holds together tightly, the relationship of each idea to previous ideas made clear as the composition unfolds. Coherence is especially important in writing that analyzes ideas and attempts to persuade others of the reasonableness of a point of view. There are three basic relationships in all analytical writing: AND relationships, BUT relationships, and THEREFORE relationships.

AND relationships. **Much of your writing involves adding one idea to another. A composition about the rise in crime, for example, might include a number of specific examples of such crimes: an elderly couple mugged and beaten, a young girl raped, a house broken into and looted. Each of these examples would have an AND relationship to the others; you would be saying, structurally, "There's this *and* that *and* the other thing."**

BUT relationships. **BUT relationships show contrast and signal the turning from one side of an argument to another. For example, you may say, "I agree that the police should not have full power to do as they wish when apprehending criminals. *But* I believe they must have sufficient freedom of action to do their job effectively." Here you would be saying structurally, "On the one hand, there is this; on the other hand, that."**

THEREFORE relationships. **THEREFORE relationships signal the drawing of a conclusion. You might, for instance, write this passage: "The man had been tried and convicted of assault three times previously. He was in the vicinity of the assault that took place that night. And he had no alibi. *Therefore,* the police department's decision to interrogate him was justified." The word *therefore* signals that what follows is a conclusion about what has preceded.**

If you want your compositions to be effective in expressing your reasoning to your readers, it is not enough to reason well; you must also provide the signal words that will make the logical relationships between your thoughts clear. Suppose, for example, a dialoguer had expressed the idea that John Hinckley's attempt to assassinate Ronald Reagan was no different morally than the plots to assassinate Adolf Hitler, and that to be consistent a person must either condemn both attempts or approve both. You might evaluate that view as follows:

> **It is true that the attempt on Reagan's life was essentially the same act as the attack on Hitler's life: an attempt to snuff out the life of another human being without warning, where the would-be killer served as judge, jury, and executioner. *But* the circumstances in which the acts took place were dramatically different. Hitler was a dictator who, though constitutionally elected, took away the people's freedoms. Reagan, on the other hand, whatever his personal faults and limitations, conducted his presidency within the law. *Therefore,* it is not inconsistent at all to judge the attempts on their lives differently.**

The use of *but* and *therefore* here clarify the logical relationships of the ideas and prevent misunderstanding. Such clarification is, of course, not only necessary in brief analyses like the one above, but in detailed ones as well. In fact, because length and complexity tend to increase the chance of misreading, such clarification is even more important in longer analyses.

In choosing the best words to signal the relationships between your thoughts, you are not limited to the three basic words. There are a number of other words and phrases you can substitute for them. Here are the main ones:

> To add information (AND): also, first, second, next, further, another, still another, next, similarly, finally, moreover
>
> To make a contrast (BUT): however, nevertheless, yet, or, on the other hand, in contrast
>
> To draw a conclusion (THEREFORE): so, for this reason, consequently, in conclusion, thus, accordingly, as a result, if . . . then

Occasionally you will need more than a word or phrase to express a relationship. In such cases, use one or more sentences. For example, you might find it helpful to say, "All the arguments we have examined so far have serious weaknesses. But there is another argument, one that avoids these weaknesses. . . ."

SAMPLE COMPOSITION

Here, together with the dialogue that prompted it, is a composition that illustrates the value of clarifying logical relationships:

The Dialogue

HAROLD: I didn't vote in the last election. Did you?

GORDON: I wouldn't waste my time voting. Politicians all lie anyway, so you can't believe what they say.

HAROLD: I agree. Even if they are honest to begin with, they become crooks when they take office. They have to play the political game or they won't get the support of the party.

GORDON: I used to think that independent candidates were the ones to support. But they usually don't have a chance to get elected running against the major parties. And even if they did get into office, they'd have no backing or cooperation, so they couldn't be effective.

The Composition

The Lesser Evil

The ancient Greek eccentric Diogenes, the story goes, set out to find an honest man. Though he conducted his search in broad daylight and with the aid of a lighted lantern, he was disappointed. Diogenes' modern counterparts, Harold and Gordon, share that disappointment, at least about politicians. Judging from the numbers of people who fail to exercise their voting privilege even in major elections, Harold and Gordon are not alone in their view.

All words used to signal important relationships between ideas are italicized. (If you look closely, you will find some additional, unitalicized signal words marking relationships of less importance.) Note how each adds clarity to the presentation and helps readers avoid misunderstanding.

Presumably Harold and Gordon have evidence for their position: promises made and broken by politicians, perhaps, and documented cases of misuse of office. Such evidence, unfortunately, can be found in abundance at every level of politics. *But* does that evidence justify the conclusion that there are no honest politicians? *And* even if that conclusion were reasonable, would it suggest that voting is a waste of time? These are important questions. Harold and Gordon, *however,* and those who share their view, seem to ignore them.

Harold agrees with Gordon that all politicians lie *and thus* can't be believed. *Yet* he suggests that some politicians are honest when they gain office and are later corrupted. This is a contradiction. *If* these politicians conduct honest campaigns, *then* they are not lying politicians when the voters make their choice. *Similarly,* it is not clear what made Gordon support independent candidates in the past, but he appears to have regarded them as honest. (His comments about them refer to their inability to be effective, but not to dishonesty.) *Yet* he says they all lie.

Moreover, both men's references to dishonest politicians are sweepingly general. They appear to be working at the level of assumption and speculation. At least there is no indication that they have wondered whether they have enough real cases of dishonest politicians to support such generalizations, or whether the cases they have in mind are typical.

But even if we overlook the inconsistency and lack of restraint, Harold and Gordon's argument is seriously flawed. Even if every candidate for political office were dishonest, there would still be a good reason for voting: to elect the *less dishonest* candidate, and so ensure that government would be less corrupt than it might otherwise be. *In conclusion,* Harold and Gordon's view is based on an immature view of the world. Not every situation affords us a choice between good and evil; sometimes our only choice is between the greater and the lesser evil.

DIALOGUE EXERCISES

Analyze each of the following dialogues as you did the dialogues in previous chapters. In addition, look for errors in reasoning and keep them from influencing your judgment. Then write a composition on one of the dialogues, presenting and supporting your view of the issue and applying the writing tip given at the end of the chapter. Note: Be sure your composition goes beyond merely discussing errors and deals thoroughly with the larger issue.

1

Note: In two separate cases, the U.S. Supreme Court ruled that the use of trained dogs to detect drugs is legitimate under certain circumstances. In the first case it ruled that citizens' rights are not violated when dogs are used to sniff airport luggage if police have reason to suspect that drugs are present.[2] In the second case, it approved the use of dogs to sniff students' lockers, cars parked on school property, and students themselves when they are suspected of drug possession. However, it outlawed the use of dogs for mass searches of students.[3]

LARRY: What's the difference between searching somebody and searching everybody? Wrong is wrong. And the use of dogs in any search is an outrage. Man's best friend, hah!

MABEL: Something has to be done about the drug problem. The pushers are even peddling in grade schools now. I think the use of dogs to detect illegal drugs is a creative way to enforce the law. It doesn't hurt anyone but the creeps who bring misery into others' lives.

LARRY: It hurts more than pushers. It hurts drug users too. Kids have free will—they have the right to choose what substances they will or won't take. Anyway, the Supreme Court has no right to judge any case involving drugs.

MABEL: Why not? They're the highest tribunal in the country.

LARRY: Because they're a bunch of old fogeys, that's why. What do they know about drugs? If they'd ever puffed a joint, they'd have croaked. They're hypocrites, too. Notice that they don't let dogs sniff out their scotch and gin at airports. But young people's drugs—that's a different matter. They make me sick.

MABEL: How can you get so angry about their doing their job of interpreting the law according to the Constitution?

LARRY: That shows how much you know about the Constitution. It guarantees every citizen freedom from unreasonable search and seizure. Now I will admit that having dogs sniff luggage at airports is a legitimate way to keep foreign drugs from entering the country. But searching lockers and cars and students is a violation of a fundamental right.

2 ______________________________

OONA: Jake said that he hates Anna.

GLADYS: I was there when he said it. He was very angry at the time. He'd just failed an important test. Besides, he'd been drinking just before he blew up at her. I'm sure he didn't mean what he said.

OONA: The reasons you mentioned for not taking him seriously are exactly why I believe he meant what he said. Psychologists say that the truth comes out at such moments. Both stress and drinking lower inhibitions and break down the disguises people put on to mask their feelings.

3 ______________________________

TRUDY: Some of the sex acts depicted or referred to in today's books and movies are really perverted.

WERNER: The concept of perversion is old-fashioned. When you say something is perverted, you are really saying nothing more than "It doesn't turn me on."

TRUDY: That's not what I'm saying at all. I'm saying certain sexual behavior is disgusting whether it turns someone on or not, and if anyone is turned on by it, he or she should see a psychiatrist.

WERNER: Sex behavior depends on a person's preference, nothing else. "Different strokes for different folks," as the saying goes.

TRUDY: Are you serious? Do you mean to say that chains and whips and black boots and humiliation are normal?

WERNER: They're not the norm, the standard most people adhere to, but then the majority of people don't eat artichokes either. I'm saying if both partners favor sado-masochistic pleasures, then those pleasures are legitimate—normal, if you will—for them.

TRUDY: If you follow that reasoning, you have to endorse child molesting and bestiality.

WERNER: That's absurd. Those activities have nothing to do with what we're talking about.

4 ______________________________

Note: The Television Information Office, an organization financed by the television industry, has issued a six-page research paper arguing that television is not the cause of declining reading scores in the nation's schools. The research paper claims that children's reading scores have more to do with "socioeconomic factors" than with the amount of television they watch, and that heavy viewing doesn't cause reading problems but is the result of those problems. It states, "Children having difficulty with classroom study and with homework will turn to television . . . precisely because of their reading difficulties."[4]

OMAR: It's got to be a phony research study.

LEIGH: How do you reach that conclusion?

OMAR: What would the television industry say? Surely not that television is responsible for reading difficulties. They have to say television is good for us, or else we might stop watching it and they'd lose money.

So they make up a bogus research study, or maybe they hire some spineless professor to do it for them.

LEIGH: But maybe the evidence does point that way. Maybe independent researchers have reached the same conclusion.

OMAR: If they have, you can be sure it's because the TV big shots paid them off. Think about it for a minute. What type of people are in the TV industry? Slick Madison Avenue types who'd sell their mothers for a few rating points. People without consciences who write catchy jingles to sell us products that don't live up to their promises. People who worship the dollar bill.

5 ______________________________

Note: An Arkansas seventh-grader accused of stabbing a playmate to death said that shortly before the stabbing he had watched a horror movie, Friday the 13th, *on television. The movie depicted people's throats being cut.*[5]

DANIELLE: A terrible thing, to be sure. But at least some good will come out of it.

NELSON: What do you mean?

DANIELLE: For years the debate has raged over whether violence in the media is responsible for the increase in real-life violence. Now at last we have indisputable evidence that it does. Moreover, once this case is publicized, people are bound to be aroused enough to exert pressure on the media and eliminate violence.

6 ______________________________

ED: Some philosophers say the essential struggle in human life is between the individual and society. Others say it is between the individual and himself or herself. Which do you think it is?

MAX: I think it's between the individual and himself or herself. Each of us has good tendencies and bad. You might say each of us is two selves in one. Those selves are usually in conflict—if we yield to the higher self, we grow in understanding and wisdom, develop our capacities, and make a positive contribution with our life. And if we yield to the lower one, we wallow in past mistakes, watch our potential waste away, and devote ourselves to trivial pursuits.

ED: I say the essential struggle is between the individual and society. The shaping force of society is so powerful, particularly in our formative years, that the way we respond to it largely determines what we do with our lives. Will we conform to group standards or develop our own? Will we accept society's values and patterns of thinking and acting, or will we assert our individuality? Will we be mired in our culture or transcend it? The answers to these questions—all of them reflections of the struggle with society—determine the quality of our existence.

7 ______________________________

Note: One of the least publicized "sports" in the United States is dogfighting. Though they are illegal in most states, dogfighting matches draw as many as 500 spectators, many of them gamblers betting on which specially trained dog will maim or kill the other.[6]

NORA: Some sport that is. Anyone who would train an animal to destroy other animals is a monster. People like that should be jailed for life. And people who watch such matches don't deserve much better treatment.

PAUL: How do you know such people are monsters if you have never met them? Maybe they're good citizens and loving parents. And what right do you have to condemn a sport if you've never witnessed it yourself?

NORA: I don't have to attend a match in order to know that it causes pain and suffering to the dogs, any more than I have to stick my hand into a fire to know that fire burns. Besides, the Humane Society has condemned dogfighting, and it's illegal in most states. That should tell you something about how harmless it is.

PAUL: What it tells me is that there's no end to people's hypocrisy. Those bleeding-heart types are always ready to cry and wring their hands over the slightest imagined hurts to animals, but they're remarkably silent when it comes to human pain and suffering. Where were they when Hiroshima was bombed? And why aren't they protesting the slave-labor camps in Russia today? Those are the real evils, not the contests held to see whether one dog is stronger or more aggressive than another.

8 ______________________________

Note: In November 1982, a Connecticut man who had been arrested and charged with four rapes and released on bail each time was arrested on yet another rape charge. The judge released him on bail.[7]

PATTI: And just what did the judge think the pervert would do when he was released, volunteer his time to counsel rape victims? I'll tell you what he probably did—went right out looking for another woman to attack.

RAMON: You have no way of knowing that. People do repent and reform their behavior, you know. But even if he still had the same criminal tendency, the judge was right in letting him free on bail. A person is innocent until proved guilty!

PATTI: Setting a rapist free on bail is like shooting a missile off without aiming it—you may not know where it's going to land, but you can bet it will cause tragedy wherever it does.

RAMON: Not at all. It's like going out of your way to help someone you don't like, not because you want to help him, but because you know it's the right thing to do.

9 ________________________________

Note: In 1972 and then again in 1982 the City Council of Evanston, Illinois, considered a proposal to tax the students of Northwestern University to offset the cost of unpaid services provided by the city. The Association of American Universities opposed the proposal, which they believed would serve as a lamentable model for other college communities.[8]

KIM: It's certainly not a popular idea on college campuses, but it does make sense. If local government provides a college with sewer and water lines, fire and police protection, and other services, the college should pay. It's not right to expect the local taxpayers to pay.

TOM: Why not? Taxpayers pay school taxes even if they have no children. The idea behind that tradition is that everyone benefits from the education of his or her neighbors, so the cost of education should be shared by everyone. The same principle should apply in this case.

KIM: College is different. It goes beyond the minimal educational level needed for the preservation of society. So the people who receive the benefit, college students, should pay for it, not the general public. I certainly wouldn't be thrilled if this city levied a tax on the students at this college, but I wouldn't complain if they did, either. It's a sensible idea.

TOM: Come on now. You know as well as I do that college towns take advantage of students. The merchants take all they can but give as little as they can get away with giving in return. Just the other day you complained to me about the attitude of the clerks in that department store in the mall.

10 ______________________________

EPHRAIM: I can't understand why we Americans continue to tolerate such giveaways as welfare and unemployment benefits when they are driving the country to financial ruin.

BERTHA: They are hurting us, to be sure, but we have no reasonable alternative to them. People have to have food, shelter, and clothing. And if they can't find work, the government has to provide for them.

EPHRAIM: Do you really believe that nonsense about there not being enough jobs? There's a job for everyone who wants to work. The problem is that the welfare bums don't want to work. Why should they exert themselves when they can sit on their butts and live better than the rest of us?

BERTHA: Hey, my dad was laid off a few years ago when the automobile industry was hurting, and he's no lazy bum.

EPHRAIM: I didn't say he was. His case is the exception that proves the rule. I know an entire family in my hometown, all of them able-bodied, yet none of them work. They sit around all day, drinking beer and smoking cigarettes paid for by my family's tax dollars. If our country's ever going to recover economically, we've got to eliminate the welfare system. It's either lighten the load on the boat or watch it sink.

11 ______________________________

Note: The Princeton University instructor found that the honor student's senior thesis had been lifted nearly word for word from a book, so he reported her to the appropriate student-faculty committee. The committee decided to withhold her degree for one year and to notify the law schools to which she applied of their disciplinary action. The student took the matter to court but lost.[9]

GRACE: That's a terrible penalty to pay for copying a little from a book. The committee was grossly unfair.

AL: Yeah. It happens all the time. I know I've copied that way more than once and all my friends do it. You have to borrow ideas from books when you do term papers; how else can you get enough words to meet the length requirement? And if you footnoted every borrowed idea or put quotes around borrowed phrasing, the whole paper would be one big footnoted quotation.

GRACE: That professor must have been out to get her. There's no way he couldn't have known when he assigned the paper that students would be plagiarizing. I'll bet if he'd wanted to, he could have nailed most of the students in his class for the same offense. What I can't figure is why the court didn't come down hard on the university.

AL: It's the establishment thing. You know, the university and the court system are part of the establishment, so one watches out for the other. Students are outsiders, so they don't count. They have no rights.

GRACE: I blame the professors too. They never teach you how to avoid plagiarism. They just warn you about it. That's no help at all.

12 ______________________________

Analyze and respond to the dialogue that began this chapter as you have done with the dialogues above.

5 Identifying Assumptions

GERTRUDE: The evidence is clearer than ever that people aren't responsible for their actions and therefore society shouldn't hold them responsible.

HEATHCLIFF: I don't know of any evidence that supports that conclusion.

GERTRUDE: It's now known that fetuses can be adversely affected if during pregnancy their mothers smoke, drink, take drugs, or don't get proper rest and nutrition. It's also known that children can be seriously harmed if parents neglect them, make them feel inferior, or abuse them physically or psychologically. So if people act antisocially or criminally later in life, it's unfair to blame them. Their parents are to blame.

THE OBVIOUS error in Gertrude's reasoning is overgeneralization. She extends her statements about certain fetuses and certain children (the unfortunate ones whose parents do not care for them properly) to people in general. Before she can legitimately make such a generalization, she must establish that criminals in general typically come from the background she describes.

Overgeneralization is not, however, the only error in Gertrude's reasoning. She also makes the assumption that people are powerless to rise above the circumstances of their prenatal and early childhood experiences. Even though she does not express this idea, we can be sure she has it in mind because otherwise she would have no reason to say it is unfair to blame wrongdoers. Gertrude's assumption is unwarranted. Despite the fact that some harm done to fetuses and children is irreversible, there is ample evidence that people can frequently rise above their early conditioning, given the motivation to do so and the encouragement of others.

WHAT ARE ASSUMPTIONS?

Assumptions are ideas that are taken for granted. That is, they are ideas people have in mind before they are conscious of them and their influence on the reasoning process.* Because assumptions exist without people's awareness, they are not found directly expressed in dialogues (or in writing). Instead, they are *implied.*

There is nothing necessarily wrong with making assumptions. It would be impossible to conduct our daily affairs efficiently without them. Most of us shut off the alarm clock and get out of bed in the morning without checking to see the time; we merely assume it is the time we set the alarm to go off, rather than three hours later or earlier. Similarly, we assume that hot water will still flow from the hot water faucet, that our car's gas tank will not be empty when the gauge reads full, that when our traffic light is green the light on the street to the right of us is red, and that our college campus has not been turned into a sausage factory without our knowledge. In such situations, assumptions serve a useful purpose —they free our minds from thinking about remote possibilities unnecessarily.

HOW ASSUMPTIONS AFFECT REASONING

Yet despite the usefulness of assumptions in everyday affairs, they can create obstacles to critical thinking when they occur in the consideration of complex issues. Even when they are warranted (justified), assumptions exert an influence over people's thinking that is independent of their conscious thoughts and thereby reduce their control over the reasoning process. Moreover, many assumptions are unwarranted. Unwarranted assumptions are formed arbitrarily, without justification, in matters about which there is reasonable ground for disagreement. They take *too much* for granted and so introduce errors into people's thinking without their awareness.

To appreciate more fully the harm that unwarranted assumptions do to people's thinking, let's borrow an analogy from mathematics. Imagine a calculator that not only registered the figures entered into it, but occasionally entered an additional figure of which the person was unaware. Such a calculator would be worse than worthless; it would place all the person's calculations at the mercy of caprice. Fortunately, the harm

* Scientists sometimes use the term *assumptions* in a special way: as a synonym for *hypotheses,* possible conclusions that are carefully formulated and then tested for confirmation or denial. But that is a different use from the one that concerns us here.

done by unwarranted assumptions, unlike that done by an aberrant calculator, can be avoided if we learn to recognize and deal with them.

SOME COMMON UNWARRANTED ASSUMPTIONS

Each of the following unwarranted assumptions occurs quite commonly in dialogues. Although a few are listed here for the first time, most are variations of errors discussed in earlier chapters. Keep in mind that their occurrence as assumptions is different from other occurrences because assumptions are implied, but not expressed.

***The assumption that people's senses are always trustworthy*.** **The five senses, and particularly the two dominant ones, seeing and hearing, are people's contact with external reality. It would be difficult to overestimate their importance. But the fact that they are important does not mean that they are perfect. At best people's seeing and hearing are subject to physical limitations: the distance from which they are observing; the obstacles created by noise, brightness, and darkness; and so on. In addition, there are psychological limitations. Because perception is influenced by people's states of mind, what they see and hear is sometimes distorted by what they *want* or *expect* to see and hear. Accuracy of the senses is something to strive for but should not be taken for granted.**

***The assumption that having reasons provides assurance that reasoning has taken place*.** **This assumption is no more sound than the assumption that having money proves that it has been earned. (Money can be begged, borrowed, or stolen, as well as earned.) Reasons may be developed by careful analysis and evaluation or simply be borrowed uncritically from what others say. People are daily exposed to a constant stream of ideas from direct contact with others and from the media. These ideas slip quietly into the mind. Then days, weeks, or months later, when conversation creates a demand for reasons, memory recalls the borrowed ideas and they spill out of the mind as thoughtlessly as they entered.**

***The assumption that conviction constitutes proof*.** **It is common for speakers to assume that the more strongly they hold an idea, the better the idea must be, and that ideas they are absolutely convinced about are for that very reason true. Even casual examination of this assumption reveals it is unwarranted. We all know examples of situations in which other people—and, yes, we ourselves—have been passionately committed to ideas later found to be mistaken. Error, it seems, has no respect for people's convictions. In fact, it is more likely to be found where feelings are strong because it is precisely there that people tend to be uncritical.**

***The assumption that familiarity is the measure of validity*.** **This assumption may take any one of several forms. One is "Whatever I like must be good**

because I like it." Another is "If I've heard it a number of times before and never objected to it then, it must be acceptable now." A third is "If I have been taught or told this by people I love and respect—for example, parents, teachers, or friends—and have believed it for a long time, it must be so."

This assumption is unwarranted in all its forms. Because human beings are imperfect, it is possible for people to be taught, and thereby become familiar with, shallow, prejudiced, and outright fallacious views. If they never look beyond familiarity in evaluating ideas, they can never hope to escape their errors. The only sensible measure of ideas is how well they fit reality. Whether they are familiar or unfamiliar is irrelevant.

***The assumption that if one event closely follows another in time, it must have been caused by the other.* This assumption appears in discussions of causes and effects. Part of its appeal lies in the fact that in many actual cause-and-effect relationships, there is a closeness in time. Lightning flashes and thunder roars, the second phenomenon a direct effect of the first. Nevertheless, what is so in *many* situations is not necessarily so in *all* situations. If someone's car breaks down several hours after she let a friend use it, it would be wrong to assume the friend's using it caused the breakdown. Similarly, if a period of inflation follows a new president's taking office, it would be wrong to assume the new president has caused the inflation to occur.**

Would it be wrong to consider the possibility that the friend has done something to the car or that the president has mismanaged the economy? Not at all. In fact, critical thinking demands that all significant possibilities be considered. But that kind of analysis is conscious and careful. Assuming is neither.

***The assumption that if the majority believes something, it must be so.* This assumption would be harmless if there were some magic in majority thinking. But there is no such magic. The majority may believe something because it is the most reasonable view or merely because it is popular. History provides countless examples of situations in which the majority view was not only wrong but disastrous. The execution of witches and the practice of slavery are two examples of practices condoned by majorities. Careful thinkers concern themselves not with how many people accept a view, but with the quality of the arguments for and against it.**

***The assumption that the way things are is the way they should be.* The influence of reality on people's thinking is strong. This is generally good but not always so. The fact that a condition or state of affairs exists is sometimes taken for *justification* of its existence. Take, for example, the fact of poverty. Some people assume that because it now exists and seems always to have existed, it must be a natural human condition that it would be foolish or misguided to try to eliminate. If this assumption were warranted, then it would be foolish to search for the causes of disease, to**

try to prevent war, and to campaign against drunken driving and drug abuse. No, the fact that a condition or situation exists in no way reflects on its value. Good situations and bad exist side by side, and responsible, conscientious people try to distinguish between them, strengthen the former, and overcome the latter.

RECOGNIZING SPECIFIC ASSUMPTIONS

The assumptions we have been considering are common enough to warrant special mention. Nevertheless, they are not the only assumptions you will encounter in dialogues. Many others will occur, and in such variety that it is impossible to classify them all. Yet you will have no difficulty identifying any assumption if you develop the habit of being alert to the full meaning of the speaker's words, and wherever any part of that meaning is not expressed directly, asking "What is the speaker taking for granted here? Is he or she warranted in doing so?" Let's examine some dialogues and see how this approach would work:

GERTRUDE: I read recently about a man who gave up a $50,000-a-year job as an airline copilot to open a Skid Row bakery in Los Angeles to help the poor. He makes so little money in the bakery that he has to paint houses on weekends to support his family.[1]

HEATHCLIFF: You say he was making $50,000? I can't understand some people. They achieve success in life and then toss it away for some idealistic dream.

Heathcliff is assuming that making a good salary is synonymous with being successful. Since there are other ways of measuring success (personal satisfaction and the effects of one's actions on others, for example), this assumption is unwarranted.

GERTRUDE: Did you hear about the creative approach a California man used to get more people to vote in the 1982 elections? He organized a ballot-stub sweepstakes. Voters sent in their stubs and a drawing was held for $5 million in prizes, including cameras, clothing, and even a date with "Dynasty" star Linda Evans.[2]

Heathcliff: Five million dollars. Wow! That guy must either be a drug pusher or the son of an oil sheik to have that kind of money to throw away.

Heathcliff is assuming that the man who developed the approach paid for the prizes himself. Since there are other ways of financing sweepstakes, his assumption is unwarranted. (In the actual case referred to here, the principal financing was done by donations.)

GERTRUDE: Here's an unusual case for you. A rape victim killed her attacker in self-defense and then sued his estate for damages for trespass, assault, false imprisonment, and rape. The Minnesota Supreme Court upheld her right to sue.[3]

HEATHCLIFF: I'd think it would be enough for her to take the guy's life. That's the ultimate penalty for a crime. Suing his estate makes his heirs pay for his misdeeds. And somehow that doesn't seem fair to me.

GERTRUDE: It was established that he committed the crimes she's seeking damages for. Therefore she's entitled to sue even though the man is dead.

The assumption made here is somewhat more subtle than the assumptions made in the foregoing examples. Gertrude's second speech reveals the assumption that the offenses the man committed and the harm they did are the only relevant considerations in the case, that his death in no way diminishes their significance. This assumption, unlike the ones above, is warranted. (Gertrude's argument would, of course, have been more persuasive if she had been aware of this assumption and expressed it directly.)

As important as it is to be alert for other people's assumptions in dialogue, it is equally important to be alert for them in your own thinking about issues. You can do this by using the following approach: Whenever you are considering important issues, discipline your thinking more than you ordinarily do. Whereas in everyday situations you may permit yourself to assume many things in order to work more quickly and efficiently, when you are formulating your view of an issue, take nothing at all for granted. And once you have finished formulating your view, take an extra moment or two to "read between the lines" to find assumptions you were unaware of. Remember that assumptions do not only corrupt other people's thinking. They will corrupt yours as well if you do not guard against them.

WRITING TIP: STIMULATE YOUR READERS' INTEREST

So far in this chapter we have discussed unwarranted assumptions that cripple *thinking* about issues. Now it's time to discuss an unwarranted assumption that cripples *writing* about issues. That assumption is that your readers will be interested in what you write simply because you wrote it. It is an easy assumption to make; your ego will deceive you into making it if you allow it to. The truth, however, is that your readers will be too absorbed in their own thoughts to be interested in yours automatically. If you want them to be interested, you must stimulate their interest.

There are two broad ways to stimulate reader interest. The first we noted in the introduction: to be exact, economical, and lively in your expression. (If you have relaxed your effort toward that end in recent weeks, renew it now.) The second way is to be imaginative in designing titles, introductions, and conclusions. Titles and introductions are of special importance because if they fail to arouse interest, your readers may never get to the body of your composition, let alone to your conclusion. No matter how brilliant your insights about the subject of abortion may be, if you title your composition "Abortion" and introduce it by saying "Abortion is a very controversial issue . . ." or "This composition is about the subject of abortion . . ." your readers may read no further.

Choosing the Title. **The purpose of the title is to get the readers' attention and stimulate their curiosity. The best titles are eye-catching, informative, and easy to remember. Jot down title possibilities for later consideration whenever they occur to you, but never decide on a title until after you have finished your rough draft. In addition, never use the general topic of the composition as your title. A dozen compositions written about a particular issue will share the same topic, but their titles should all be different, each reflecting the uniqueness of the treatment. Remember that the more titles you consider, the better your choice is likely to be; so invest some time and brainstorm the possibilities.**

Choosing the Introduction. **The purpose of the introduction is to transform the readers' curiosity into interest and to engage their minds, preparing them for the body of your paper. In persuasive writing, where many readers will oppose your view, the introduction should also establish a basis of agreement. Accordingly, focus on points your readers will be less likely to dispute, leaving more controversial points until the body of the paper. Similarly, refrain from expressing your thoughts in a way that will make your readers defensive because their first reactions may be difficult to overcome.**

Choosing the Conclusion. **The conclusion serves to reinforce the controlling idea and bring the composition to a satisfying close. (It should never introduce new ideas and leave them undeveloped.) Reinforcing means reminding readers of the controlling idea but not necessarily restating that idea in the same words. In fact, although direct repetition is acceptable in longer compositions, it indicates a lack of imagination and is often offensive to readers. As a rule, it is better to echo the controlling idea, expressing it in different words, than to restate it. There are, of course, other ways of concluding, such as comparing your judgment with one or more other judgments to show the greater reasonableness of yours or discussing the positive effects to the issue your approach would produce.**

Each of the sample compositions in preceding and subsequent chapters has an effective title, introduction, and conclusion. Spend a few minutes now and examine them to see how they stimulate the readers' interest and enhance the ideas in the compositions.

SAMPLE COMPOSITION

Here is a composition written in response to the dialogue that opened this chapter. Note in particular how the title, introduction, and conclusion reflect the considerations discussed in the writing tip.

The Composition

Accountability or Chaos

Hatred, scorn, deprivation, physical assaults, sexual abuse—many criminals have experienced all of these at the hands of their parents. Often the neglect and even sadism begin before birth, in the earliest stages of fetal life. For centuries the damaging effect of such horrible experiences was not fully understood. Today we know that those experiences can sow the seeds of hostility that later burst into antisocial behavior; so it is understandable that we ask, when dealing with criminals, "What factors in their childhood may have prompted them to criminal behavior?"

The title reflects the controlling idea: that we must not abandon the concept of accountability because without it there would be social chaos. The list of strong words in the introduction has dramatic impact and thus transforms the readers' curiosity into interest.

However, when we become too absorbed in this question, we tend to focus our attention too narrowly and miss other important considerations. This narrow focusing, I believe, explains the permissive attitude toward criminals that developed in the 1960s and 1970s.

There are so many influences at work in people's lives that it is difficult to know the exact combination of causes that underlies a particular action. For one thing there is the problem of determining whether the person was obeying or disobeying his or her conscience and whether acting freely or under strong pressure (perhaps to the point of compulsion). We know from experience that it is possible to resist both conscience and pressure. For example, on one occasion, we may overrule conscience, not because of any pressure, but because we want to. Yet at another time we may experience extreme pressure from our desires as well as from other people and yet resist.

For another thing, the exact motivations that lead us to act are sometimes unclear. Did we steal the candy bar from the grocery store at age nine because we were angry at our parents for denying us dessert, because we wanted to eat what our friends ate, or because we wanted to "beat the system"? And was our cheating on the high school examination a simple act of desperation, a refusal to accept the consequences of our failure to study, or rebellion against our parents' moral code?

If we cannot be certain about such matters in our own lives, how can we expect to be certain of them in the lives of strangers? We can't. So we shouldn't focus only on the factors in the childhood of criminals that may have influenced them. We should also consider these questions: Did the criminals know their actions were wrong? Were they acting under compulsion or did they have a choice of behaviors—that is, could they have behaved differently if they had wanted to?

Such considerations help balance our concern over the possible negative influences in criminals' childhoods. That balance is imperative. Without it, we risk abandoning the foundation of our justice system, the notion of people's accountability for their actions. Without that notion a society is only a step away from social chaos.

Note that the full presentation of the controlling idea in this composition is reserved until the final paragraph. This is effective only because the title and the second paragraph point directly to the controlling idea and ensure that the reader will not be confused.

DIALOGUE EXERCISES

Analyze each of the following dialogues as you did the dialogues in previous chapters. In addition, identify all significant assumptions and determine whether they are warranted. Then write a composition on one of the dialogues, presenting and supporting your view of the issue and applying the writing tip given at the end of the chapter.

1

CARLA: Sex education has no place in the schools. It causes more problems than it solves.

BEATRICE: That's ridiculous. Ignorance is the real villain. When people don't know the facts about sex, venereal disease and unwanted pregnancies increase. Knowledge is the key to responsible sexual behavior.

CARLA: You're wrong and I can prove it. Our parents and grandparents had no sex education in school and the number of cases of venereal disease and unwanted pregnancies in their day was only a fraction of the number today. The more widespread sex education has become, the higher the rates have risen.

BEATRICE: How can sex education possibly be related to the increase in venereal disease and unwanted pregnancies?

CARLA: Simple. It dignifies the subject of sex and encourages kids to talk about it. It puts ideas in their minds and, as everyone knows, the thought is father to the deed.

2 ______________________________

Note: A born-again Texas businessman and a television evangelist smashed $1 million worth of art objects and threw them into a lake after reading the following verse from Deuteronomy in the Bible: "The graven images of their gods shall ye burn with fire: thou shalt not desire the silver and gold that is on them, nor take it unto thee, lest thou be snared therein: for it is an abomination to the Lord thy God." The objects, which belonged to the businessman, were mostly gold, silver, jade, and ivory figures associated with Eastern religions.

CECIL: That's a real measure of faith, the willingness to discard earthly treasures out of spiritual conviction.

ELLIE: It's more like an act of lunacy. It's a terrible waste of wealth. If he'd wanted to express his religious conviction, he could have done something to help his fellow human beings.

CECIL: By doing what?

ELLIE: He could have sold the objects, taken the million dollars, and given it to the needy of the world. Or he could have donated it to a religious organization or a hospital. Instead, he threw it away and helped no one.

CECIL: You don't understand. Selling the objects would have corrupted others. He's a religious man. The Bible told him what to do, and he had no choice but to obey.

3 ______________________________

AMOS: Parents and teachers are forever saying "Don't be a follower. Think for yourself, assert your individuality, be a leader." But, you know, that's a lot of bunk.

ERIC: I've always considered it good advice. It's not just parents and teachers who say it. A lot of books are written expressing the same view. What makes you reject it?

AMOS: It's dishonest. The whole of society is based on the idea that there are not only leaders and followers, but more followers than leaders. Businesses have supervisors and subordinates, the armed forces have officers and enlisted men and women. In the home parents have responsibility over children. Even in the church, there are higher and lower offices. It's a cruel deception to tell people they can be leaders when in fact most of them are going to be followers. It would be a lot fairer to teach them to accept the inevitable—the fact that their lives will in most cases be inferior.

4 ______________________________

Note: In May 1982, a Long Island woman became the first person convicted under a New York State law prohibiting harassment with ethnic or racial slurs. She was sentenced to spend thirty-five hours in community service for using an anti-Semitic obscenity against a neighbor.[4]

VERA: The sentence was appropriate. The crime was minor, but real nonetheless, so some punishment was called for.

WINIFRED: There shouldn't be any punishment at all. In fact, the law should be repealed. It's an infringement on the right of free speech.

VERA: Come on, now. The Constitution doesn't say anything about the right to insult one's neighbor.

WINIFRED: It doesn't have to *say* it explicitly. It *means* that. If I want to call someone a wop or a nigger or a "polack," or, as in this case, a kike, I have every bit as much right to do so as you do to call someone a hero or a philanthropist. Either way it's an exercise of free speech.

5 ______________________________

Note: A Miami high school student earned all A's in her academic subjects but was kept off the honor roll because of a C grade in conduct. Her father, an attorney, took the school to court to get her listed on the honor roll.[5]

HARVEY: Too many parents defend their kids when they don't deserve defending. The father would do his daughter a favor if he made her take her punishment for acting up in school.

FAITH: I disagree. School officials should be held accountable for their ridiculous rules and regulations. In my school you had to have 90 percent or better attendance in order to qualify for honor roll. Isn't that absurd? This case is similar. Unless the school has a formal course in etiquette, that *C* in conduct shouldn't be a factor in determining who's on honor roll.

6 ______________________________

ISAAC: Did you read that letter in "Dear Abby" from the woman whose son announced he was taking his fiancee's name when they got married?[6]

GERRY: You've got to be kidding. What did Abby say about it?

ISAAC: She said the son was an adult and free to make up his own mind, so the woman should accept his decision with grace.

GERRY: That's lousy advice. I'd tell the son if he wants publicity that badly to do something worthwhile, not something bizarre. And I'd add that he's starting out his marriage on the wrong foot by giving in to his wife's demands that way. Marriage should be a partnership.

7 ______________________________

Note: When the new $60,000 faculty dining room opened at State University of New York, Binghamton, students protested that it would be used exclusively for faculty and administration. If State University funds are used, students reasoned, then everyone on campus, including students, should be able to use the facility.[7]

LLOYD: The students were right. It's time students were treated as professors' equals. Special dining facilities, preferred parking, private study rooms in the library, special book-borrowing privileges—it's as if faculty were royalty and students were peasants.

JACK: Yeah. It's like something out of the Middle Ages. And what's even worse, it happens in *public* colleges and universities. It's bad enough in private institutions, but public institutions are tax-supported, and with the economy unstable, frivolous spending is an affront to the taxpayers.

8 ______________________________

Note: In 1982 the New York State Legislature dropped the requirement that rape victims must offer "earnest resistance" to the rapist in order for prosecution to take place, but added the provision that the force used by the rapist must cause in the victim "fear of immediate death or serious physical injury."[8]

PIA: In other words, those lawmakers were saying that no crime takes place when a woman is raped unless she fears death or serious injury.

MORT: In the technical sense, that's right.

PIA: Are those lawmakers for real? When a woman doesn't want to have sex and a man makes her do so anyway, that's rape. It shouldn't matter whether he threatens her with a submachine gun or simply overpowers her. It's still a violation of her body and should be treated as a crime.

MORT: You're oversimplifying. There are cases where the woman says no and really means yes, and cases where the woman says yes and then later decides she really should have said no. There are even cases where a woman is excited by the rapist's advances and, though she initially protests, actually derives sexual pleasure from the act. There has to be some test the courts can apply to separate those cases from real rapes. I believe the "earnest resistance" approach is the best test, but if that's unacceptable, then the "fear" test will do.

PIA: With that kind of thinking you qualify for a seat in the state legislature.

9 ______________________________

Note: An Indianapolis man filed a $12 million lawsuit against the R. J. Reynolds Tobacco Company, charging that their advertising deceived him into thinking that cigarette smoking would not harm him. Subsequently, he became addicted to smoking and suffered physical damage.[9]

MARCIA: Three cheers for that man. The tobacco industry has led millions of people into smoking with their phony ads that make it look so glamorous. I hope the court awards him every penny of the $12 million.

OLIVER: I don't see how he can sue one tobacco company. They all advertise the same way. How can he be sure that he wasn't more influenced, subconsciously, by another company's ads? And I wonder whether he has any way of proving that he smoked only Reynolds Company cigarettes. I'll bet the case is thrown out of court.

MARCIA: I'm surprised at you. Here you are supporting the tobacco industry when you know that smoking does untold harm to people.

10 ______________________________

NIGEL: Know what's the biggest problem in this society? The fact that parenthood is regarded as a right and not as a privilege.

RAISSA: I'm not sure what you mean. Isn't parenthood a right? After all, people have always been free to decide whether to have children. And that's not just the case in this society. It's the way it is in most societies. I don't see any problem about that.

NIGEL: The problem is that the wrong people often choose to be parents. That's why there's so much physical and emotional neglect of children. People don't know when they decide to have a child what the demands of parenthood are and whether they can meet them. By the time they find out, it's too late—they've got a son or daughter and are well along in the process of screwing up his or her life.

RAISSA: It happens, sure, and a lot more often than most people realize. But what can be done about it? You can't issue licenses for having children and make it a crime to have one without a license.

NIGEL: Why not? Oh, I know it *sounds* weird, but really, why not? If I had my way, I'd have mandatory courses in parenting from grade school through high school. Beginning courses would help students understand that babies need a lot of love and attention. Later ones would focus on child psychology and the demands of being a parent. In addition, I'd require that people pass those courses before they'd be allowed to have children.

11 ______________________________

Note: In 1982 local adoption officials were directed by New York State Social Services officials not to reject applicants solely because they are homosexual or have a history of alcoholism or drug abuse, a criminal record, a dependency on welfare, or a severe emotional or physical handicap.[10]

TYRONE: That's just ducky. Now we're going to let homos have little children to practice their perversions on, criminals have apprentices to train, and people who can't fit into society themselves take on the responsibility of preparing others for adult life.

PERCY: I always thought adoption agencies screened people to determine that they were normal before letting them adopt. I wonder why they are letting down their standards now.

TYRONE: Obviously it's part of the liberal influence in government: gay rights, criminals' rights, misfits' rights, and similar crap. No good will come of it, I'll tell you that.

PERCY: I don't see how it can. Kids need foster parents who can provide for them and can show them the right way to live.

6 Forming a Judgment

REX: There's been a good deal of talk lately about the backlog of cases straining the court system. But no one has mentioned the obvious cure for the problem: to regard accused criminals as guilty until they establish their innocence.

MARIE: But what about the legal tradition of "innocent until proved guilty"?

REX: That idea was conceived when society was simple and the crime problem wasn't nearly so extensive. Today that tradition is putting an intolerable burden on the state, and the result is that justice is not being done and criminals are preying on law-abiding citizens.

As important as are the tasks we have examined in the last three chapters—making important distinctions, recognizing errors in reasoning, and identifying assumptions—they are only the preliminary part of the critical thinking process. The essential part, the part to which they inevitably lead, is forming a judgment. In the analysis of dialogues, a judgment is a conclusion about the issue arrived at after careful consideration of all relevant matters, both expressed and unexpressed.

THE NECESSITY OF JUDGMENT

Forming a judgment is seldom an easy task. There is always an element of risk present, a chance that we will reach the wrong conclusion. And the more important and complex the issue, the greater that risk is, and the greater our temptation to avoid judgment altogether. Yet succumbing to that temptation is not only a cowardly response, but an unrealistic one.

However much we might want to avoid judging, in a great many cases it is impossible to do so, because *not judging is a kind of judgment.* The opening dialogue in this chapter is such a case. If we attempt to avoid judging the issue by refusing to comment on Rex's idea, our silence implies endorsement, and the practical effect is little different than it would have been if we'd said, "I agree." Avoiding judgment when the evidence permits it is irresponsible. To adapt an old saying, all that is necessary for bad ideas to triumph is for people to remain silent when they hear them.

The best way to overcome the temptation to avoid judging difficult issues, and at the same time to gain confidence in judging, is to develop a responsible and systematic approach to judgment. The rest of the chapter will help you do this.

HOW TO FORM A JUDGMENT

It is a mistake to regard the process of judging as cold, mechanical, and devoid of feeling and imagination. Even if it were possible to make it so (and it is probably not), it would be inadvisable. Strong feelings can add vitality to our thinking. All that is necessary is that we refuse to accept them uncritically, but instead subject them to the tests of relevance and reasonableness. Similarly, as we will see, imagination can help us break out of habitual, narrow perspectives if we learn to control and direct it.

There are four steps to follow in making judgments. Let's identify them first and then take a close look at each.

1. Consider alternative arguments to those expressed in the dialogue.
2. Compare all arguments and make a preliminary judgment.
3. Assess the implications and consequences of your judgment.
4. Modify your judgment, as necessary.

Considering Alternative Arguments

Considering alternative arguments is important with all dialogues but is especially so with dialogues in which only one side of the issue is presented (that is, where the dialoguers agree). It is the only way you can be sure you have not overlooked a significant perspective, as can happen easily when the argument is subtle or when your sympathy for one point of view compromises your objectivity.

Consider, for example, this situation. The Educational Testing Service (designers of the Scholastic Aptitude Test) decided to invalidate the scores of four New Jersey high school students after another student reported they had cheated on the exam. The students appealed the decision in court, but a superior court judge upheld it.[1] Now if you were analyzing a dialogue discussing the fairness of invalidating the students' scores, and your sympathy were strongly with the students' position, you might be inclined to regard the issue as settled. In order to consider alternative views, you would have to force yourself to keep an open mind.

Here's how to open your mind to alternative arguments. List every argument you can think of concerning the issue, no matter how incorrect the argument may seem to be at that moment. Be sure to include arguments on all sides of the issue. If you have difficulty doing this, remind yourself that inability to think of any argument but the one you prefer is usually not a sign that the issue is clearcut but that you are not putting your imagination to work. Make a special effort to put aside your preferences and think as people you disagree with would think. Write down those thoughts. At this stage don't cross out any argument you have listed. (This will prevent your subconsciously "stacking the deck" in favor of the view you prefer.)

To see the value of considering alternative arguments, let's consider a case that made national headlines some time ago. The incident occurred in a New Bedford, Massachusetts, bar. A young woman started to leave when four men grabbed her, threw her on a pool table, and repeatedly raped her in full view of fifteen or twenty bar patrons. Instead of intervening or calling the police, the patrons allegedly cheered the rapists. When the incident was publicized, sensitive people everywhere were outraged. One of the responses designed to prevent such shameful behavior from occurring again was the proposal of a Massachusetts state legislator. She introduced a bill making it a crime for people not to report witnessing a felony.[2]

Now if you were analyzing a dialogue addressing the question of whether the proposed law was a good one, you would probably be inclined to ignore opposing arguments and endorse the proposal without qualification. That is a perfectly natural reaction, one surely shared by most people. But it is not a reaction that is consistent with responsible judgment. Therefore you should force yourself to go beyond it and consider what arguments might be raised in opposition. Here are two such arguments:

> Not every felony is as obvious as the New Bedford rape. It is possible for a crime (kidnapping or car theft, for example) to occur without bystanders realizing that it is a criminal act. It would be unfair to hold people responsible in such cases.
>
> Witnesses to a crime may have reason to fear for their safety or the safety of their families, if they report what they saw. It is unreasonable to make people choose between protecting themselves and obeying the law.

Comparing Arguments and Making a Preliminary Judgment

Occasionally you may find an argument that fits the facts so well and is so reasonable that it should be endorsed without qualification and the other arguments should be dismissed. More often, however, several arguments will have merit. In such cases you would form your judgment to reflect that fact. Your judgment of the proposed Massachusetts law, for example, might be as follows:

> **The law making it a crime for people not to report witnessing a felony is a good law as long as it excludes cases where the felony could reasonably have been interpreted as a lawful act and cases where the witnesses had good reason to fear that reporting the felony would jeopardize the safety of themselves or their families.**

Your preliminary judgment needn't be highly refined in its phrasing. You will have an opportunity to revise it later. However, it should be based *exclusively on the evidence* and not any prior notion of what the answer would or should be. It is natural enough to prefer conclusions that bolster the ego and leave your cherished notions undisturbed. But it is foolish to pretend that such an approach to judgment produces the most reasonable views. The test of whether a judgment is sound is not whether it fits our wishes but whether it fits the facts.

Assessing Implications and Consequences

In assessing implications and consequences, you consider what would happen if your preliminary judgment were to prevail and decide whether that would be beneficial or harmful. Your imagination is your primary tool here, as it was in step 1. Use it to construct likely scenarios. Here's how to proceed. Let's say the issue is what would be the most effective response to drunken driving. Your preliminary judgment is that second offenders should have their cars confiscated and sold and the money placed in a special fund to aid the victims of drunken driving accidents.

Using your imagination you construct this scenario (among others). A problem drinker with a wife and three small children is convicted of drunken driving for the second time and his car is confiscated and sold. The man can no longer drive to and from his favorite bar, but neither can he drive to work. Nor can his wife drive him! As a result he may lose his job and have to go on welfare.

In assessing these consequences you decide that your preliminary judgment is unsound. Although confiscating and selling drunken drivers' cars does punish them, it also punishes their (innocent) families. In addition, it creates the risk of at least some offenders' becoming tax burdens on society.

It is difficult to overstate the importance of assessing the implications and consequences of your preliminary judgments. When you fail to do so, you may create larger problems than the ones you are seeking to solve. Occasionally, you will worsen the very conditions you hope to overcome. This was the case, according to some authorities, when the idea of "no-fault" divorce was introduced. One of its intended effects was to ensure that the settlements wives received would be more equitable than they had been in the past. But the actual effect has been to work against the interests of women by lessening their settlements.[3] If the originators of the idea of no-fault divorce had been more thorough in their assessment of consequences, they might have modified the idea and realized their aims.

Modifying Your Judgment

Whenever your assessment of a judgment reveals weaknesses in it, you should revise the judgment to eliminate them. In addition, if your judgment is presented as *certain,* but your assessment reveals that it is only *probable,* then state it as probable. And if you find it applies not in *all* situations but only in *some,* specify where it applies and where it does not.

The aim of modifying your judgment is to make it even more reasonable in finished form than it was in preliminary form. The key to achieving this is to realize that slight variations in wording can make a significant difference in meaning and to choose your words with great care. Let's say your judgment concerns the credibility of the Reverend Sun Myung Moon's testimony in federal court that he had not only talked with Moses, Buddha, and Jesus, but also that Jesus had approached him for assistance in "the salvation of the universe."[4] Assuming your reaction to Moon's claim was skeptical, you might consider either of the following expressions of your view (among other possibilities):

> **Moon's assertion is ridiculous; he certainly never spoke to any of the three individuals, and Jesus surely didn't ask him for help in the salvation of the universe. It is impossible to converse with people who are no longer physically present on earth.**

> **Moon's assertion is at best difficult to accept because there is no way to test its accuracy. If he expects thinking people to believe what he says, he should offer them some documentation other than his claims that these extraordinary conversations took place. The burden of proof is his.**

Despite the fact that these statements express very similar views, they are very different in one important respect—their reasonableness. The first expresses certainty where there is only probability and manages to convey an attitude of scorn for all religious experience, an attitude that borders on dogmatism. The second, on the other hand, though no less forceful in its challenge to Moon's claim, takes a position the majority of religious believers and nonbelievers alike would find reasonable.

There are two other tasks to perform when you are modifying your judgments. The first is to check to be sure you have defined all important terms clearly enough that they will not be misunderstood. If, for example, you were discussing the question of discipline in the schools, you would make sure you explained what kinds of discipline you had in mind (scolding? withholding privileges? assigning extra work? corporal punishment?).

The second task is to check to be sure that you provided all appropriate qualifications. Saying something *should be* is different from saying it *should be under certain conditions.* The absence of such a qualification can make an otherwise sound judgment unsound. In checking your judgments for appropriate qualifications, consider the following kinds:

> Qualifications of time: Does it really happen all the time (or never)? Or does it happen usually, often, sometimes, occasionally, infrequently, or at some specific time?
>
> Qualifications of place: Is it really everywhere (or nowhere)? Or is it in most places, many places, some places, a few places, or in some specified place?
>
> Qualifications of certainty: Is the idea absolutely certain? Or is it only probable or possible?
>
> Qualifications of condition: Does it happen (or should it be done) in all circumstances (or no circumstances)? Or, instead, in most cases, many cases, some cases, a few cases, or under certain specified conditions?

WHEN TO RESERVE JUDGMENT

So far we have focused on situations in which the evidence is complete and compelling enough to permit a judgment to be made. There are, however, other situations, in which prudence dictates that you refrain from making a judgment, at least at that time. By learning to recognize them, you can avoid irresponsible judgments and the embarrassment they cause.

When exactly should you reserve judgment? Whenever you don't know enough about the issue to make a responsible judgment. Determining when you lack sufficient knowledge can be difficult. If you are like most people, you will often have strong feelings about, and therefore want to address, issues you know too little about to judge responsibly. You will need sensitivity and wisdom to realize when that is the case and self-restraint to act on that realization.

This direction about reserving judgment is not an invitation to avoid judgment. Once you have determined that you lack sufficient knowledge, the next appropriate step is to investigate the issue and obtain the necessary information so that you can make a responsible judgment. (Exactly how to conduct your investigation most efficiently is explained in detail in the next chapter.)

WRITING TIP: EXPRESS YOUR JUDGMENT CAREFULLY

Many writers make the mistake of assuming that because they had a judgment clearly in mind before or while writing, they necessarily expressed it clearly in the composition. It is not only possible to have a judgment clearly in mind and then fail to express it—in many cases such failure is likely. Once the mental act of making a judgment is completed, it quickly becomes a past event. Five seconds, minutes, or hours later, the desire to have expressed the judgment can make us remember having expressed it whether we did so or not.

To ensure that your judgments take place on paper as well as in your mind, adopt this three-part strategy. First, record all your thoughts on paper from the moment you begin addressing an issue; let no significant thought occur without writing it down. This may seem a time-consuming requirement, but it doesn't have to be. You can write quickly, roughly scribbling sentence fragments just legible and complete enough for you to decipher later. Second, when you later evaluate your notes and form your judgment as detailed in this chapter—considering and comparing alternative arguments, assessing the implications and consequences of your preliminary judgment, and modifying that judgment accordingly—do all your thinking on paper as well as in your mind. Finally, when revising your composition, look for passages in which you have left a judgment implied rather than directly stated. If you find any such passages, revise them to make your judgments explicit.

Here are two examples of the directness and clarity with which you should express your judgments. Each is taken from a sample composition from a previous chapter. (You may wish to examine sample compositions from other chapters for additional examples.)

From Chapter 2

I believe that teachers do students a disservice when they assign no homework, tolerate lateness and inattention, and give B's and A's for substandard performance. And when they allow students to call them by their first names, they invite disrespect. . . . I definitely believe there should be more required courses; more homework; more demand that students master such basic skills as spelling, grammar, arithmetic, and penmanship; and tighter graduation standards. In short, I believe there should be less self-discovery and more self-improvement.

From Chapter 4

But even if we overlook the inconsistency and lack of restraint, Harold and Gordon's argument is seriously flawed. Even if every candidate for political office were dishonest, there would still be a good reason for voting—to elect the *less dishonest* candidate and so ensure that government would be less corrupt than it might otherwise be. In conclusion, Harold and Gordon's view is based on an immature view of the world. Not every situation affords us a choice between good and evil—sometimes our only choice is between the greater and the lesser evil.

SAMPLE COMPOSITION

Here is a sample composition, together with the dialogue that prompted it, further illustrating the careful expression of judgments.

The Dialogue

SAM: There seems to be a lot written today about workaholism. But I'm puzzled about what's being said.

EVELYN: What's workaholism?

SAM: Working extraordinarily hard at your job, so hard that you can be considered a work addict.

EVELYN: So what are you puzzled about?

SAM: My father and grandfather have always taught me that laziness is the affliction for which work is the cure. Now everyone seems to be saying the reverse. Work, it seems, is the new villain.

EVELYN: I know you have great respect for your father and grandfather, but their ideas seem a little dated.

The Composition

Hard Work: Curse or Blessing?

Workaholism is a popular subject today. Articles and books are written, warning people of the danger of working too hard, driving themselves to greater levels of achievement, being overly productive. For example, Wayne Oates, who coined the term *workaholic* and wrote *Confessions of a Workaholic,* argues that the stress of workaholism is linked to a number of physical afflictions ranging from colds to heart attacks to ulcers, as well as to the psychological disorder known as manic-depression.

These warnings may very well be necessary for those who overwork to the point of neglecting other important duties, such as to family. Yet there is good reason to regard the warnings with dismay and a measure of suspicion.

This passage and the other underlined passages in the composition are the author's judgments. Note that each is not only carefully qualified to meet the test of reasonableness, but also sufficiently clear and direct that the readers needn't guess at the author's meaning. (Note, too, the care with which the author blends judgments and evidence to achieve a persuasive presentation.)

The tendency to work too hard and long is, of course, an extreme behavior and is properly rejected on that account. Nevertheless, that tendency poses far less danger to individuals or to society today than its opposite, sloth, the tendency to work too little and without enthusiasm. A number of educational commissions have decried the "rising tide of mediocrity" in the nation's schools. Numerous social critics have lamented the decline in craftsmanship that has resulted in shoddy products and services. Studies have shown time and again that a large number of workers hate their jobs. And experts in business and industry blame the decline in creativity and productivity for the loss of this country's competitive edge in the world market. Each of these problems is either caused or aggravated by negative attitudes toward work.

The work ethic is not a fad that was embraced capriciously by psychological misfits. It is a central theme of Western civilization. Honest labor has historically been regarded as noble, uplifting, and pleasing in the sight of God. Some, in fact, have regarded it as a form of prayer. In this tradition empty hands, like the proverbial idle mind, have been regarded as the devil's playthings.

The most honored men and women in our history have dedicated themselves to higher goals than relaxation, or an integrated personality, or even good health. Leonardo da Vinci was a prodigious worker, sometimes going from sunrise to sunset without pausing to eat or drink. Benjamin Franklin involved himself in not one or two but a half-dozen careers. Thomas Edison proclaimed that genius is 99 percent perspiration and 1 percent inspiration. And George Bernard Shaw, a prolific writer, once credited his achievement to the fact that he learned how to work ten times harder than he was formerly used to working.

It is possible, of course, that such people were merely addictive personalities, lacking in philosophical perspective, caught up in the compulsion of defying their own and the world's better judgment. But it is more likely that they enjoyed a vision of the inestimable value of excellence that our generation has lost, a vision that books and articles warning us not to work too hard will scarcely help us to regain.

DIALOGUE EXERCISES

Analyze each of the following dialogues as you did the dialogues in previous chapters. Take special care in forming your judgment. Then write a composition on one of the dialogues, presenting and supporting your view of the issue and applying the writing tip given at the end of the chapter.

1 ______________________________

Note: Many states have taken measures to make it more difficult for drivers under age eighteen to get, keep, or use their licenses. Among the restrictions that have been adopted or are being contemplated are the following: a longer written test, a longer waiting period before issuing a license to those who pass the test, stricter penalties for traffic violations, and the suspension of driving privileges between midnight and 5:00 A.M.[5]

BERNARD: It's discrimination; that's what it is.

SPIRO: Not really. Teenagers are the least skilled drivers and they're involved in a disproportionate share of accidents.

BERNARD: I don't believe that's so. But even if it is, it's wrong to punish all teens for what a few have done.

SPIRO: It's not a punishment. It's a precaution, and everyone benefits from it.

BERNARD: That's just what the government said when they rounded up innocent Japanese-Americans and stripped them of their rights after the start of World War II.

2 ______________________________

Note: A high school anatomy class in Agoura, California, dissects human cadavers as well as cats and frogs. The teacher obtains the bodies from a university medical school.[6]

SARAH: Positively disgusting. It makes my skin crawl even to think of it.

AUSTIN: There's nothing wrong with the practice. They do it in medical school all the time. Only the squeamish object.

SARAH: They have to do it in medical school to train doctors. But high school isn't medical school. It's the supreme act of indignity to a human being—to dissect his or her body in a school classroom.

AUSTIN: Don't get so moralistic. The bodies are those of homeless derelicts, I'm sure, or wards of the state.

3 ______________________________

Note: A study of how strongly people in Europe and America endorse the Ten Commandments revealed that a majority on each continent believe the Commandments apply fully to modern life, but that some Commandments (for example, "Thou shalt keep the Sabbath holy") are not as widely endorsed as others. The study also revealed that the overall percentage of Europeans who believe the Ten Commandments apply is considerably smaller than the percentage of Americans.[7]

EDITH: That's called the statistical fallacy.

AGATHA: What are you talking about?

EDITH: The idea that whatever a majority of people believe must be so because they believe it is called the statistical fallacy. The majority *can* be wrong, you know.

AGATHA: But how can you find out what is and what isn't applicable as a guide to living except by determining what people actually live by?

EDITH: You're mixing apples and orangutans. With the Ten Commandments there isn't anything to determine. They apply for all time and it doesn't matter whether people accept them or not.

4 ______________________________

Note: In past decades college officials debated whether to censor student newspapers that published stories containing four-letter words and explicit sexual references. In the 1980s the debate continues, but the issue has changed. Some student papers are publishing articles that make fun of blacks, women, and homosexuals. And others are urging students to paint graffiti on campus buildings and take up shoplifting to combat conformity.[8]

ERNEST: Such articles may be childish and tasteless, but that's no reason to censor them.

GEORGINA: Are you kidding? Minorities pay good money to go to college. And on most campuses, I'm sure, their student activity fee pays for the student newspaper. Where's the fairness in charging them for articles that insult them or that encourage lawbreaking, which ultimately costs them as taxpayers?

ERNEST: Why is everything a money issue with you? So a buck or so from every student's activity fee goes to the newspaper. Big deal. That doesn't give every student the right to play fascist and set editorial policy. The articles are written in a spirit of fun or for shock value. Censorship is not the answer. If a pesky fly buzzes around your head, you don't fire an elephant gun at it. Well, maybe *you* do, but no sensible person does.

5 ________________________________

Note: In Meridian, Michigan, a husband and wife bought movie tickets for their children, ages five to twelve, and then left them alone at the theater. The theater staff refused them admission because the film was rated R, *thus requiring them to be accompanied by their parents. Subsequently, the couple sued the theater, charging violation of the youngsters' civil rights.*[9]

CARLOS: I hope they won that lawsuit. Who are the theater people to tell them what they can do with their own children?

WILLA: That's not the point. The theater staff had no reasonable alternative to obeying the law.

CARLOS: There are too many laws today telling us what we can do and what we can't do. Our society's becoming more repressive all the time. The parents here were saying, "Hold it—you've gone too far. If we want our young children to see *R*-rated, or even *X*-rated, films, then that's our business and our business alone. Government can keep its nose out."

WILLA: Any parents who would let little children see *R*-rated films ought to have their heads examined.

CARLOS: You may have a right to think whatever you want but not to push it on others.

6 ______________________________

Note: High school administrators around the country are using a new weapon in their fight against student drinking during school hours—a pocket-sized breath tester called "AlcoCheck." The device is similar to those used by the police.[10]

HOWARD: I wonder how they use that device. Do they just stand in the hall, see a kid stumble, and force him or her to submit to a breathalyzer test?

RUTH: How else could they do it? They must do something like that.

HOWARD: Talk about schools being like prisons. This beats everything. Imagine the embarrassment, the humiliation experienced by the kid who's naturally a little clumsy, or the kid who wanders a little while walking down the hall because she's thinking deeply about her lessons, or the one who just likes to act goofy once in a while for fun.

RUTH: That's right. And even the kid who does drink in school has a right to his or her privacy. School officials have no right to invade that privacy, no matter how noble their intentions.

7 ______________________________

CAROLINE: White people really have the cards stacked against them in the job market today. Affirmative Action programs make sure that blacks and Hispanics get favored treatment.

ROSE: Then how come blacks and Hispanics have more than double the unemployment of whites? And how come there are so few of them who have made it into the middle class economically?

CAROLINE: Because they lack initiative. To say it more bluntly, because they're lazy. I know we aren't supposed to say that anymore. It's not polite, but it's true.

ROSE: Affirmative Action programs and minority quota systems were set up to overcome our society's history of discrimination against minorities. The reason for their joblessness is not that they don't want to work; it's that they weren't allowed to work. And by the way, *women* are minorities, too, and are covered by the same programs.

CAROLINE: I support programs that give women a fair shake. They've been oppressed by chauvinism since the beginning of time.

8 ______________________________

Note: In June 1982, the U.S. Supreme Court ruled that presidents cannot be forced to pay monetary damages for violating the rights of Americans.

The specific case in question involved Richard Nixon's allegedly illegal firing of a civilian Air Force worker who had disclosed to Congress that a military plane project could cost $2 billion over official estimates. The majority opinion of the Court stated, "We hold that [Nixon], as a former president of the United States, is entitled to absolute immunity from damages liability predicated on his official acts."[11]

ASA: I'm afraid that ruling gives a little too much power to the president, certainly more than the framers of the Constitution intended.

PEG: Isn't it necessary to free presidents from worrying about the ripple effects of their decisions so that they can do the job more effectively? I mean, if presidents had to worry about possible lawsuits every time they made official decisions, they would never make any decisions.

ASA: This was not a ripple effect. It was the main consequence of a direct act; a malicious act, I might add. The Supreme Court's decision says, in effect, that the president is beyond the reach of the law.

9 ______________________________

KEITH: I can't understand current emphasis on early childhood training. People are reading to their children and playing music for them to hear while they're still in the womb. And once the child is born, the emphasis on nurturing intensifies.

EMILY: How can you object to that? The start a child gets in life can make all the difference in what he or she becomes as an adult.

KEITH: I don't *object* to what is done. I just don't understand it. It certainly can't hurt to do all those things that are associated with nurturing, but it can't help much either. It's too late to make much difference at that point.

EMILY: Too late when the child is in the womb? That's absurd.

KEITH: It's elementary biology. Once conception occurs, the genetic package is complete. Every detail of that person is indelibly encoded in that package, from sex to eye and hair color to height and basic metabolism. To pretend that it can be changed is to deceive ourselves. We are essentially what our genes program us to be.

10 ______________________________

LILLIAN: Do you think parents should be told when their teenage daughters are given birth control devices by doctors?

ROY: Absolutely. Parents are responsible for their children until they become of age. They have a right to be told.

LILLIAN: I'm not as sure as you. I can see how not telling them is a violation of their rights as parents, and the family has been weakened enough today without weakening it further. But on the other hand, teenage girls are not just objects. They're people, and as such they have rights, such as the right to determine how their bodies will be used. And many times they can't talk to their parents about sex.

ROY: Nonsense. Parents care about their kids. They have their interests at heart more than anyone else, particularly some money-grabbing doctor. If kids really want to talk to their parents, there's nothing stopping them—except the possibility that they don't want to hear what their parents will say.

LILLIAN: Another thing bothers me, too. Why does the issue always focus on teenage girls rather than teenage boys?

ROY: Check with your local anatomist.

7 Investigating the Issue

CLAUDIA: I read an interesting book last week that claims psychotherapy makes few significant changes in a patient's life. It's titled *The Shrinking of America* and was written by Bernie Zilbergeld, a psychologist. He argues that talking to a sympathetic friend is often as helpful as, and considerably cheaper than, a trip to a psychotherapist.

BARNABY: Does he make a convincing case? How have psychologists and psychiatrist's reacted to the book?

CLAUDIA: I was impressed by his argument. Some of his peers were, too. But many dismissed the book as sensational and biased.[1] That doesn't surprise me, though. Given its message, the book was bound to receive a negative reaction from many people in the field.

IS ZILBERGELD's claim legitimate? Is the argument he advances a sound one? In order to answer these questions responsibly, we'd first have to read the book and consider both the argument and the evidence offered to support it. Unless we had some background in psychology, however, reading the book would not be enough. We would have no basis for deciding whether any important evidence was omitted and whether the evidence offered permitted a different interpretation from the author's. To develop that basis for deciding, we'd have to investigate further.

Sensitivity to the need for further evidence and willingness to admit ignorance and postpone judgment are prerequisites of effective investigation of issues. But those qualities are not in themselves sufficient to ensure success in investigating. It is also necessary to know what to look for and how to go about looking. Let's examine each of these subjects in some detail.

WHAT TO LOOK FOR

The object of investigating issues is to obtain evidence; that is, information that contributes to the formation of a judgment. There are four broad classes of evidence:

Confirmed Details or Statistics

The emphasis here is on the word *confirmed.* This kind of evidence is the least subject to error or the distortion of individual perception. It consists of factual matters about which there is general agreement among knowledgeable people, and which may usually be found in the library. How many drug-related deaths were there in the United States last year? What percentage of our taxes is spent on defense? What is the present rate of illiteracy in Montana? What does the Eighteenth Amendment to the U.S. Constitution concern? The answers to these questions are examples of confirmed details or statistics.

Your Own Experience and Observation

Personal experience and observation include anything that has happened to you and anything you have witnessed happening to others. It is the one kind of evidence about which you can speak with authority regardless of your lack of scholarly credentials. And the fact that it is firsthand testimony gives it special force. (This does not mean, however, that your experience and observation are necessarily of the highest quality. You may, for example, have perceived selectively or carelessly.)

The Judgments of Authorities

Authorities are people who possess expert knowledge. They are not only familiar with their subject but also in command of it. They have gotten beyond superficial knowledge, penetrated the complexities of the subject, and come to terms with its intricacies. This, of course, does not place them beyond the possibility of error. Even the most respected experts can be wrong. What, then, is the difference between experts and amateurs? Experts are less likely to err than amateurs. And when they do err, their errors are seldom gross or common; rather, they occur in a framework of valid ideas. Therefore, their testimony—and their judgments—are more trustworthy than those of others.

This is not to say that experts always agree. No field is without its areas of dispute, and it is not uncommon to find several competing theories or interpretations, each with a sizable number of advocates. Therefore, the effectiveness of this kind of evidence depends on the number of authorities who accept it and their eminence in the field. A judgment shared by virtually all respected people in the field would be more persuasive than one shared by a small number of relatively unknown persons.

Other People's Experience and Observation

Other people's experience and observation differ from yours in that you do not know them firsthand, but only from the reports of others. They may have told you directly or indirectly (for example, through a third party or through a medium such as magazines or television). Obviously, this kind of evidence is riskier than the other kinds because it leaves more opportunity for rumor and error to creep in. Any time you use it you should be reasonably sure of the veracity of your sources and the accuracy of the report. You would naturally put more trust in a reliable person than an unreliable one, a careful reporter than one given to exaggeration, a critical-minded person than a rumormonger. Similarly, you should be more skeptical of secondhand and thirdhand reports than of firsthand observation.

How can you tell when you have enough information to end your investigation? Because no field is ever completely closed to new discoveries or new inventions, in one sense investigation should never end. Still, we seldom have unlimited time at our disposal; practical necessity demands that we make decisions and take action. The following guidelines reflect this reality:

> ***End your investigation when you have obtained sufficient information to frame a judgment that is certain.*** **Wishing, assuming, or pretending that a judgment is correct does not constitute certainty. Certainty exists where there is no good reason for doubt, no basis for dispute. It is rarely attained, especially in controversial issues.**

> ***End your investigation if you find that certainty is unattainable, yet you have obtained sufficient evidence to establish that one view of the issue has the force of probability.*** **This means, in other words, that you can demonstrate the reasonableness of preferring that view to other possible ones. Remember that demonstrating reasonableness is very different from merely asserting it, and that you must identify and evaluate all possible views before you can reasonably prefer any one.**

HOW TO FIND EVIDENCE

Finding evidence is often thought of as a dull, plodding enterprise, but it doesn't have to be that way. It can be enjoyable, even exciting. To make it so, you need only understand more fully the resources at your disposal and have a plan for using them systematically and imaginatively. The plan we'll examine has three steps: consult your experience and knowledge, interview authorities, and visit the library. It is designed to obtain the evidence you need to form a judgment about any issue and to do so quickly and easily.

Consult Your Experience and Knowledge

This first step of consulting your own experience and knowledge may seem too obvious to mention, yet it is the one most people tend to use least effectively. Each of us possesses a wealth of information that would strain the capacity of a large computer. The problem is that we regard most experiences and items of knowledge narrowly, and so we file them away in our minds under one classification rather than all the classifications that are appropriate. For example, you may watch a favorite soap opera every day. Because it is fiction that you watch as entertainment, you classify it only that way, missing the fact that its treatment of human relationships and reactions to life warrant classification as psychology. Thus if you were investigating an issue in psychology such as the effects of carrying a grudge on one's mental health, you would never think to draw upon what you learned from years of watching soap operas.

To draw more effectively on your knowledge and experience, begin now to regard all your experiences and all your knowledge more broadly. If you are, for example, a business major and are taking elective courses in anthropology and biology, look for ways in which those courses relate to your field. In addition, be curious about the implications of what you hear in everyday conversation, read, and view on television. Here are two examples of how such curiosity can bear dividends.

> **The article occupied less than five column inches in the weekly magazine. It was titled "Success Secret" and explained how two Harvard researchers determined from a study of 456 individuals that success in adulthood is more related to a child's capacity to work than to his or her intelligence, social status, or family background.[2] Curiosity about the broader implications of this finding would suggest its relevance to education, and filing it away in your memory under that heading as well as under "guides to success" would help you think of it at some later time when you were investigating the issue of educational reform. Accordingly, you might present it as evidence that giving homework and classwork to students contributes to their effectiveness in later life.**
>
> **"Movie Led Teen to Donate Organs": This article detailed how a fifteen-year-old Texas teenager was so affected by *Thursday's Child,* a TV film about organ transplants, that he told his brother he wanted to donate his organs to others when he died. One week later, the teenager was killed when a pickup truck struck him as he was riding his bicycle. Subsequently, five people received organ transplants as a result of his generous decision.[3] Now you would obviously classify this news story as an exam-**

ple of a caring person. But if you looked beyond the obvious, you'd also classify it as evidence that television viewing is not a neutral activity, that our minds do respond, however subtly, to what we see. And this classification would help you remember the story when you were investigating the question of whether violence on television has a harmful effect on viewers. You might, for example, present it and then reason that if TV can prompt such noble reactions, it presumably can prompt ignoble ones.

In addition to being more curious about experiences and knowledge when you receive them, you should also make an effort to remember more effectively. Instead of limiting yourself to recalling material directly related to the issue, try to recall, as well, material indirectly related. Overlook nothing.

Interview Authorities

You may be thinking "The first step had relevance to me, but this one doesn't because I don't live in New York City or Los Angeles." That would be a mistake. Authorities are not found only in major cities. For most subjects there are authorities even in small villages. You may not ordinarily think of business executives as experts, but they are, and so are doctors, lawyers, real estate brokers, and insurance agents. All you need do to tap their expertise is interview them.

If you live in a college town, you have an even wider assortment of experts at your disposal. Psychologists, economists, historians, linguists, architects, musicians, philosophers—the list is as long as the number of departments on your campus, multiplied by the number of professors in the average department. For virtually any subject you are dealing with, you will be able to find someone whose training and professional experience can provide the illumination you are seeking.

When you find authorities to interview, be sure you keep in mind the guidelines basic to all interviewing:

1. Call for an appointment well in advance of the time you wish to conduct the interview. (If the person is too busy to see you in person, ask whether he or she will give you a five- or ten-minute interview over the telephone and be ready with your questions just in case the person agrees to speak to you at that time.)

2. Make yourself available at a time that is convenient to the person, arrive on time for the interview with your questions planned in advance, and don't overstay your welcome. If the person agrees, tape the interview so that he or she will not waste valuable time waiting while you take notes.

3. Avoid questions that can be answered with a simple yes or no. Instead, ask questions such as "What do you think about . . . ?" After you've asked a question, listen carefully to the answer and follow up any lead that seems promising. (Some interviewers are so busy thinking of their questions that they forget to listen to the answers.)

Professional writers use the interview frequently, often calling all around the country. How do they find out the authorities' numbers? By consulting the Yellow Pages under the field of expertise in question. (If you thought the Yellow Pages were useful only to find someone to fix your car or washing machine or to deliver pizza, you weren't being imaginative enough.)

Visit the Library

The next step in investigating the issue is to extend and supplement the evidence found by consulting your experience and interviewing authorities. Begin by examining your own personal library and the libraries of your roommates and friends. You may never have considered textbooks a valuable resource in investigating issues, but they are. A single psychology text, for example, can provide a mountain of material relevant to dozens of particular issues. Add to that the other texts found in the average college dormitory (ethics, history, sociology, economics, and health, to name just a few) and you have at your disposal authoritative material relevant to hundreds of issues. Moreover, most textbooks have detailed indexes to make your search easier.

After examining your personal library, visit the campus library. Even a small college library will usually offer the following basic research tools:

General Encyclopedias. Encyclopedias contain articles written by authorities on every significant subject of knowledge. The articles are not only brief and highly readable, but also free from bias: Where controversy exists, the authors describe it and detail the major disagreements without taking sides. There are a number of very good encyclopedias, but *Encyclopedia Americana* and *Encyclopaedia Britannica* are usually considered the best.

Special Encyclopedias. If your investigation must go beyond basic information, there are a number of special encyclopedias to serve you. For example, there are encyclopedias of religion and ethics, philosophy, law, medicine, superstition and folklore, and science and technology. These deal with their subjects in the same objective fashion as general encyclopedias, but in greater depth.

Almanacs. Almanacs provide miscellaneous facts and statistics about a wide range of subjects. Most are published annually, so that if the focus of your investigation is a particular year, you can go directly to the volume for that year. The *World Almanac* is available from 1868. Other almanacs include the *Information Please Almanac,* and *The New York Times Encyclopedic Almanac,* and *The People's Almanac* (published in three volumes).

Indexes to Periodical Literature. The best-known periodical index is *Readers' Guide,* which covers general literature. For more scholarly literature there are, for example, the *Humanities Index,* the *Social Science Index,* the *Business Periodicals Index,* and the *Art Index.* Periodical indexes provide a comprehensive listing of magazine and journal articles published during a particular year or group of years. They are designed to save you time in researching. Rather than browse at length through individual issues of magazines and journals looking for what is relevant to your subject, you need only check the listing for that subject to identify all the relevant articles, as well as the magazines they appeared in and the publication dates and page numbers.

The New York Times Index. This index is your key to locating any story written in the *New York Times* from 1851 to the present. To use it, you need only select the volume for the appropriate year and look up the subject you are investigating. When you have identified a story you wish to read in full, you simply copy down the date and page number, obtain the microfilm covering that edition of the newspaper, and place it into the microfilm reader.

Abstract Publications. An abstract publication is a compilation of all published articles and books directly or indirectly concerning some aspect of the subject. Its most helpful feature is that it offers summaries of the articles and books. The listings in an abstract publication will thus guide you to those materials you wish to obtain and read in full. In some cases, the summaries themselves will be sufficient for your purposes. Among the most helpful abstract publications are *Psychological Abstracts, Research in Education,* and *Index Medicus* (a medical research tool).

The Monthly Catalog of U.S. Government Publications. The U.S. government is the largest publisher in the world. This catalog of its publications covers works in every field, from adolescent pregnancy to professional sports, and from psychology to warfare. It includes a cumulative index.

The Card Catalog. The card catalog is your library's classification file for all its materials. It is arranged in three ways: by subject, by author, and by title. Your library will have a guide to its use, including instructions on how to read the information on the cards in file.

The Library Staff. The most important resource in your campus library is the people who work there, the librarians and their assistants. They can provide you not only with assistance in finding the research tools listed here but also with suggestions about other tools that are available. For example, if you were investigating a particular event, they might suggest consulting *Facts on File,* a weekly world news digest, or *Editorials on File,* a fortnightly collection of newspaper editorials from around the United States and Canada.

USING THE LIBRARY EFFICIENTLY

Consulting the sources described above and reading the relevant books and articles may seem like a formidable task. However, it needn't be if you work efficiently—that is, if you take advantage of the shortcuts professional researchers use. Each of the shortcuts we will discuss demands a small investment of time, but the savings in time and frustration it affords you make that investment worthwhile.

1. *Have a plan.* Decide before you begin what research tools are relevant and in what order you will use them. In some cases you will need historical data; in others, the interpretation of authorities; in still others, only current statistics. Occasionally, you will need all this information and more besides. Knowing what you need before you visit the library can spare you extra trips later.

2. *Determine what subject headings are relevant to your issue.* The most helpful information may not be classified under the first heading you think of, but instead, under some related heading. If, for example, the issue concerned thinking, some related headings would be, logic, creativity, reasoning, inference, problem solving, decision making, deduction, induction, critical thinking, memory, and cognitive processes. Although it would seldom be necessary to look up the listings for such a large number of headings, you should always consider as many possible headings as you can and then look up several of the most appropriate ones.

   You needn't rely on your creative imagination to supply the list of relevant headings. Most abstract publications contain indexes of terms. For example, *Psychological Abstracts* has the *Thesaurus of Psychological Index Terms.*[4] If you were investigating the broad classification Personality, you would find a number of related classifications, many of them with several subclassifications. Personality Traits alone lists more than seventy-five subclassifications, from Adaptability to Tolerance.

3. *Keep a record of the sources you find helpful.* Not every source you consult will prove helpful, but when you find one that does, list all publication information about it. This listing will not only provide you with the material necessary for formal footnoting and a bibliography (if that should be required); it will also save you time should you have to return to the source to check a detail. The basic publication information to include is as follows:
   a. The author's name, if it is given.
   b. The title of the work. (In the case of an article included in a larger work, such as a newspaper, an encyclopedia, or a magazine, list the title of the larger work, as well.)
   c. The volume number, if the work is published in more than one volume.
   d. The publisher's name and the year and place of publication. (In the case of a periodical, include the day or month of publication, too.)

4. *Read selectively.* Although leisurely reading has its place, as a rule that place is not while you are investigating issues, when time is an important factor. It is usually better to read one chapter in each of ten books than to read ten chapters in one book (assuming, of course, you pick the right chapters). Many books will have some valuable material about your issue but only as a small part of a larger treatment. Use a book's index or table of contents to determine exactly what is relevant to your purpose. In addition, while you are reading, be alert to research leads. If a passage refers to a helpful book, jot down whatever information is provided about the book for later investigation. Similarly, look at relevant footnotes and bibliographies for other works to consult.

5. *Take brief but careful notes.* There is no contradiction in this advice. It is important to get the information down accurately without misrepresentation. Nevertheless, it is a waste of time to write whole passages, word for word, unnecessarily. Of course, if a particular sentence is so important and so concise that you wish to copy it down exactly as it was written, then do so and put quotes around it so that you will remember that it is borrowed. But otherwise avoid writing down complete sentences. Instead, copy down only the most important details in fragmentary form. (Whenever thoughts of your own occur while you are taking notes from a source, put brackets around your thoughts so that you can distinguish them from the source's ideas later.) Write down the page number of any detail included in your notes, whether paraphrased or directly quoted.

WRITING TIP: KEEP THE EMPHASIS ON YOUR JUDGMENT

When amateurs do research, they often surrender their judgment to the authorities they consult. As the information, the interpretations, and the judgments accumulate, amateurs feel more and more humbled by the complexity they were previously only vaguely aware of. As a result, they become less confident and begin to think "What can I possibly add to all these data?" This is a natural enough reaction, but a mistaken one. The purpose of this writing tip is to help you resist that reaction, retain control of your analysis, and make your own judgments.

No matter how dependent you are on data from others, you can nevertheless stamp it with the seal of your own judgment. All you need do is apply the same critical thinking you have been using in this book to the data you obtain in your investigation. Here are four specific approaches you can take to keep the emphasis on your judgment.

1. Look closely at the ideas of each authority you consulted through an interview or through library research. Determine which of those ideas are facts and which are interpretations or judgments. Then examine the latter for weaknesses. Can you find any failure to make distinctions (Chapter 3)? Any errors in reasoning (Chapter 4)? Any unwarranted assumptions (Chapter 5)? If you find any of these weaknesses, evaluate their effect on the authority's position. Present your findings in your composition.
2. If the authorities you consult all *agree* in their interpretations and judgments, put your imagination to work and consider what objections to their view someone who disagrees might raise. Present those objections in your composition and explain whether you think they are valid objections and why or why not.
3. If the authorities you consult *differ* in their interpretations and judgments, compare their views and decide the relative strengths and weaknesses of each. State and explain in your composition which view you find most reasonable and why. If you find good reason to object to the arguments on *both* sides of the dispute, then present your own position, together with the evidence that supports it. If you find that none of the views is entirely satisfactory, then borrow from the strengths of each and construct your own view. Present that view in your composition, together with a detailed explanation of what makes it more satisfactory than the views of the authorities.
4. If you find the authorities in substantial agreement and you cannot think of any objections to their common position (a most unlikely

development if the issue you are investigating is in any way controversial), then review the characteristics of sound judgment (Chapter 6) and decide how they are reflected in the position of the authorities. Present your favorable analysis in your composition, together with any situations and cases you can think of that the authorities did not mention, but that support their judgment.

SAMPLE COMPOSITION

The Dialogue

CORNELIA: Television has the potential to be the greatest intellectual stimulant in history if those in charge of programming would use it right.

ALEXANDRA: I think it's stimulating now. This season especially there are lots of creative new shows on. I'll bet the average person learns more from TV than from books.

CORNELIA: The fact that people sit in front of the tube instead of reading doesn't mean they are being stimulated.

ALEXANDRA: I know that. I mean they learn more from that medium than from any other. In that sense it's stimulating.

The Composition

TV Dulls the Mind

In *A Parent's Guide to Children's Reading,* which won the Edison Foundation Award for its contribution to education, Dr. Nancy Larrick observed that by the time teenagers graduate from high school they have spent roughly eleven thousand hours in the classroom and twenty-two thousand hours in front of the TV set. Among the effects of all that TV viewing, Dr. Larrick notes, are shorter attention spans, diminished respect for adults, and the attitude that school is irrelevant. All three effects are more likely to hinder the life of the mind than to enhance it.

The last sentence of the paragraph is the composition author's judgment about the research findings.

No medium as large and as varied as TV, of course, could be totally without virtue. News broadcasting, shows like *60 Minutes* and *20/20* that offer in-depth analysis of issues, thought-provoking discussion shows like *Donahue,* and National Geographic special programs make a positive contribution to the minds of viewers. But such shows are the exception rather than the rule. By and large, TV is more intellectually depressing than stimulating.

The last two sentences are the author's main judgment, the controlling idea of the composition.

A brief overview of the kinds of shows that dominate commercial television will demonstrate this sad fact. The game shows that fill the daytime and early evening schedule may at first glance be thought to be intellectually stimulating, but closer examination reveals they are not. Day after day, those shows ask the same kinds of questions, questions concerning matters of fact and not matters of interpretation and judgment. Thus they reinforce a black and white "every question must have a simple answer" mentality that cripples analytical and reflective thinking. The other staple of daytime TV, soap operas, often bypasses the mind altogether and aims straight, and unerringly, for the emotions.

In this paragraph and the two paragraphs that follow it, the author's judgment is skillfully interspersed with the evidence.

Evening fare, though somewhat different from daytime programming, is no more intellectually nourishing. Situation comedies usually feature tiresome variations on comedy routines used ten, twenty, and thirty years ago on such shows as the original *Odd Couple, All in the Family, I Love Lucy,* and *The Honeymooners.* (At times it seems they also use the same laughtracks.) And the adventure series, which alternate from westerns to police shows and back to westerns, use the same dozen or so stock themes. The faces, hairdos, clothes, horses, and cars may change, but the plots and much of the dialogue remain the same. (An occasional talking animal or car is substituted, pathetically, in the name of creativity.) As if all this repetition were not enough, for almost half the year viewers are treated to re-runs!

But the worst part of television, and the most intellectually stultifying, is the commercials. Add together all the times you have had your mind assaulted by Mr. Whipple and his routine about squeezing the Charmin, that insipid fellow saying "I want to speak to you about . . . diarrhea," assorted deodorant pitchpeople, and make-believe homemakers lamenting the removal of the whitener from Final Touch fabric softener, and you have the makings of a giant Excedrin headache.

In light of all this, it should be no surprise that there are outspoken critics of TV not only outside the medium, but within as well. Ted Turner, president of Turner Broadcasting System and a TV innovator, says bluntly, "Most of the programs that get the ratings are garbage." The most damning criticism of TV programming, however, comes from the viewing public. A 1983 National Association of Broadcasters survey revealed that 49 percent of viewers are watching less TV than ever, and 63 percent claim that network programming is dull and repetitive. However much potential TV may have for intellectual stimulation, it has so far proved to be only a depressant.

The final sentence of the composition is the author's judgment. Note how it reinforces the controlling idea.

DIALOGUE EXERCISES

Analyze each of the following dialogues as you did the dialogues in previous chapters. In addition, investigate any issue for which you lack sufficient information to make an informed judgment. Then write a composition on one of the dialogues, presenting and supporting your view of the issue and applying the writing tip given at the end of the chapter.

1 ______________________________

GUY: Want to know what makes me sick? The tolerance our society has for transsexuals. I can't think of anything more disgusting than a person changing sexes to act out homosexual fantasies or to get more sexual satisfaction.

DARRELL: You obviously don't know much about transsexualism.

GUY: Don't tell me you excuse their perversion, too.

DARRELL: There's nothing to excuse. And you're mistaken in calling it a perversion. It's not.

GUY: What else can it be but a perversion? A man decides to be a woman, or vice versa. It's a mockery of nature. We are what we're born to be and it's our responsibility to accept that. It ought to be against the law to tamper with nature the way they do.

2 ______________________________

Note: Ed and Lorraine Warren are demonologists. They earn their living by researching demonology and lecturing about it to college audiences. Not only have they read widely about diabolical infestation, possession, witchcraft, satanism, and poltergeists—they have been present at real exorcisms and sincerely believe there is a devil and he is at work in the world.[5]

CONRAD: They may believe it, but I surely don't.

BARBARA: You don't deny it's possible, do you?

CONRAD: Yes, I do. I place stories of the supernatural in the same category as stories about unicorns or mermaids, as products of the human imagination. No one who lives in the age of science has any business believing in superstition.

BARBARA: Well, I do believe in it, and I consider myself as scientific in my approach to things as you are. How scientific is it, after all, to refuse to look at the evidence surrounding a phenomenon, to reject it solely on the basis that you have a doctrine against it. That's dogmatism, pure and simple.

CONRAD: There *is* no evidence.

BARBARA: That just shows your ignorance. There's a body of knowledge that has been examined and debated by scholars and experts over the centuries. Many highly respected people believe in demonic possession.

CONRAD: They must be as loony as you.

3 ______________________________

KAY: Do you make it a point to buy American? I do.

WALDO: I make it a point to buy for the cheapest price available. If that means American goods, fine. If it means Taiwanese or Japanese or Korean goods, that's fine, too. In matters financial, patriotism has no place.

KAY: People like you make it important for our government to set high import tariffs. That way, American workers are protected against cheaper imports.

WALDO: High import tariffs restrain free trade. If a country or a company can't meet the challenge of foreign competition, then they should sell out and seek a less competitive business.

KAY: American companies can meet fair competition; it's unfair competition that injures them. When competing companies in foreign countries pay their workers slave wages, they are able to sell their products cheaper than American companies can.

WALDO: You've really swallowed the propaganda campaign of American labor unions. Most foreign competitors pay their workers a fair wage and get reasonable productivity in return. Labor unions have seen to it that their workers get too much pay and do too little work. That's the real problem, and a protective tariff is not the solution.

4 ______________________________

Note: Margaret Mead, noted American anthropologist, is perhaps most famous for her Coming of Age in Samoa, *in which she argued that the comparatively primitive Samoans led happy, guilt-free, and neurosis-free lives even though they enjoyed loose family ties and casual sex. Mead's influence on public opinion was great; she is undoubtedly one of the prime movers of the sexual revolution. Yet now another respected anthropologist, who also did field work among the Samoans, has challenged her findings. He is Derek Freeman, author of* Margaret Mead and Samoa: The Making and Unmaking of an Anthropological Myth.[6]

ADRIAN: What is this guy, a publicity seeker?

ESTRELLITA: I think he's a university professor in Australia. I read a little about his book. It's not a hatchet job, but a scholarly work.

ADRIAN: But how can he attack someone as established as Mead? Her book has been required reading in American colleges for half a century.

ESTRELLITA: He says her data were all wrong. For example, she said the idea of rape is foreign to the Samoan mind and he points out that at the very time she was in Samoa, the Samoan newspaper regularly reported rape cases.

ADRIAN: But how could the bulk of her data have been wrong?

ESTRELLITA: I don't know. I think his point is that she didn't probe deeply enough to get beneath appearances, or that the Samoans themselves lied to her. Something like that. Read about it yourself and draw your own conclusion.

ADRIAN: If it's just a hatchet job, I don't want to waste my time reading it.

5 ______________________________

Note: One of the most hotly debated subjects in education today is the subject of merit pay for teachers. The subject is not a new one. The public has generally been in favor of merit pay, but teachers have traditionally opposed the idea. Nevertheless, many school systems around the country are initiating merit pay plans.[7]

LIZ: Why on earth should teachers oppose the idea of merit pay? I'll bet the ones who argue against it are the incompetents. They fear being found out.

GABRIEL: My uncle is a high school teacher and a good one. He's against it, too. He says it opens the door to too many abuses.

LIZ: Like what?

GABRIEL: I don't know. He didn't elaborate.

LIZ: It stands to reason to me that if you want excellence in anything, you have to reward it. All they'd have to do is ask the students who the best teachers are. The students always know.

GABRIEL: We could tell them, all right, if they'd only ask us.

6 ______________________________

BATHSHEBA: Have you seen Sandra lately? She's altogether different from the Sandra we knew last spring. She doesn't party anymore, she takes her studies seriously, and she's much more subdued. I don't mean she's depressed or anything like that. It's just that she's quiet and reflective where she used to be so talkative and zany.

BARTHOLOMEW: I haven't seen her, but frankly I don't believe she could have changed that much over a single summer. People don't change their personalities. We're all products of our conditioning. No stimulus is strong enough to evoke such a radically different response in so short a time.

BATHSHEBA: Whatever doesn't fit your behavioristic view of people, you reject out of hand. People can change if they want to badly enough. They can take stock of themselves, will to be different, and set about changing their habits. And many psychologists share my conviction.

BARTHOLOMEW: There is such a psychological school, but it's archaic. Behaviorists like Watson and Skinner have demonstrated definitely that the notion of free will is a myth.

7 ______________________________

Note: Bill Beausay, a psychologist specializing in sports psychology, suggests that sports be rated much as films are—X, R, or G, depending on the amount of danger and/or violence in them. He urges that children not be allowed to take part in any X-rated sport at an early age. Such sports include motorcycle and auto racing, hockey, football, boxing, and horse racing.[8]

LOWELL: Such a scheme would never work in a free country.

MARJORIE: It would if people considered it open-mindedly. It makes a lot of sense.

LOWELL: How can a boy grow up to be a man unless he takes risks and gets bruised?

MARJORIE: Always the macho routine. Have you ever read about the kinds of accidents that occur from sports where the players "get bruised"? Have you ever studied what psychologists say about the emotional effects of playing violent sports at an early age?

LOWELL: I don't have to do research. I've played so-called violent sports all my life and I'm glad I did.

8 ______________________________

Note: In 1983 the National Organization for Women (NOW) challenged a practice that had become standard in the insurance industry: charging women more for some insurance than men are charged and paying them smaller benefits than men receive. The insurance industry claims that the practice is legitimate, being based on such objective data as mortality tables.[9]

AMY: Good for NOW. It gives me a good feeling to know that there's an organization fighting unfair treatment of women.

WILFRED: NOW makes me sick. They're always griping about something or other. I think they're motivated less by a desire for justice than the urge to stir up trouble.

AMY: How can you defend the practice of charging women more or paying them smaller benefits just because they're women?

WILFRED: Look, women live longer than men as a rule, don't they? That being the case, the insurance company pays them less each year that they draw on an annuity because statistics project that the payments will have to be spread out over a longer time than men's payments. How can there be unfairness in that?

9 ______________________________

Note: In recent years a new kind of book has begun being published, the suicide manual. Such books are not bad-taste spoofs, but serious how-to guides to committing suicide. Although some hail these books as valuable aids in ending the suffering of the hopelessly ill, many find their publication disturbing. Particularly troubled are groups dedicated to counseling would-be suicides to give up the idea of destroying themselves and accept life.[10]

SETH: I can't see any useful purpose in a suicide manual. It's the one place where I think censorship is proper.

VICTORIA: I agree. Suicide attacks the most natural and deepest human urge—the urge to self-preservation.

SETH: People who want to kill themselves are emotionally troubled. No completely sane person would ever choose death over life.

VICTORIA: Imagine what would happen if such books got into the hands of children. It should be made a crime to publish or sell such books.

10 ______________________________

ROBERTA: It seems that there's more boxing on TV lately. One cable channel runs boxing shows almost continuously. I think that's terrible.

SHERWOOD: What's terrible about it? I like to watch boxing. It's an exciting sport.

ROBERTA: It's not a sport at all. There's no object to hit or catch such as a ball or puck, and no goal or basket. The whole point of the contest is to pound another human being into submission.

SHERWOOD: Just because you don't like it is no reason to attack it. I happen to regard it as the supreme battle of wits and skill. If you make a mistake, you pay for it. That's certainly more realistic than computer games. That's what you should turn your anger toward—computer games.

ROBERTA: Don't change the subject. You obviously haven't read the reports of medical authorities about the effects of boxing. You obviously haven't read the tally of young men killed in the ring. You probably haven't seen . . .

SHERWOOD: Don't tell me what I haven't seen, Roberta. I've seen a man killed in the ring. But it was an accident, and I'm not illogical enough to condemn an entire sport because of an accident.

8 Refining Your Position

OTTO: I can't believe this society's hypocrisy about gambling. Betting on horse-racing is allowed and the state even provides off-track betting parlors to make it easier. Yet betting on a professional football game or a college basketball game is a crime.

ERNESTINE: It's inconsistent, I agree. The solution, though, is not to have more legalized gambling, but less. Horseracing should be outlawed, too.

OTTO: Nonsense. Betting is a perfectly harmless activity. Every office and shop has its World Series pool, its Superbowl pool, and even its pool on how many people are going to attend the company's annual open house.

ERNESTINE: The fact that many people do something doesn't make it right; otherwise, child abuse and shoplifting would be considered acceptable.

WRITING ABOUT controversial issues usually has as its aim persuading other people that one view of the issue is more reasonable than other possible views. That aim is difficult to achieve because no matter what position you take, some part of your audience is likely to object. Consider the dialogue between Otto and Ernestine. If, after investigating and analyzing the issue, you decided that gambling should be legal, then Ernestine would object. And if you decided that it should be illegal, then Otto would object. Moreover, in either case the person whom you would most want to persuade would also be the most difficult to persuade.

The challenge of all persuasive writing is to present your position so effectively that those who disagree with you are motivated to reconsider their view. The most important step you can take to ensure that this occurs is, of course, to find the most reasonable view. All the rhetorical skill in the world is insufficient to hide a shallow view from a critical audience. Moreover, careless presentation can make a reasonable view appear unreasonable and undermine persuasion. Thus it makes sense to take the time to refine your position.

Refining your position means examining it for imperfections and complications and then revising it, as necessary, to overcome them. Few positions are ever perfect when are are first composed (if, indeed, they are ever perfect). They need modifying to fit the variety of situations that might exist and to withstand the objections of critics. And the more complex the issue is, the greater that need is likely to be. Readers who are indisposed to your views to begin with will need only the slightest reason to reject your position. The most minor flaw can provide them with that reason.

ANTICIPATING OTHERS' REACTIONS

The key to effective refining of your position is to anticipate others' reactions to it. To do this you must set aside your own perspective and view your ideas as others are likely to view them, particularly those readers whose view opposes yours. This is never easy to do. It requires that you step away from the perspective you feel strongly is the only legitimate one and view your ideas from an alien perspective. Yet despite the difficulty of this action, it is necessary because there is no other way to determine how your readers are likely to view your position.

There are two broad considerations in anticipating others' reactions: (1) *what your readers are likely to know about the subject* and (2) *where and to what extent they are likely to disagree with your view.* First let's consider the extent of your readers' knowledge.

If your readers are well-informed, you can usually dispense with background material. You can also dispense with many of the explanations, definitions, and analogies that may be necessary for the less-informed reader. On the other hand, if your readers are ill-informed, or if the subject is new to them, a great deal of background information and explanation may be necessary. Of course, the exact kind and amount of explanation required will vary from person to person. Different readers may be confused about different points. Clearly, before you can decide what to explain, define, or illustrate, you must have some idea of what your readers know about the subject.

Now let's examine the question of reader disagreement. Where your readers agree with you, they will tend to be less critical; therefore, it will take less complete and less impressive evidence to reach them. Where they disagree, however, they will tend to be more critical, and the evidence required to win their favor must be more thorough and compelling. It would be no great feat to win Otto's approval for your position that gambling be legalized, but to win Ernestine's would be considerably more difficult.

Since people's reactions are never completely predictable, you can never be certain precisely what your readers' reactions to your ideas will be. The best you can do is speculate. But speculation can be very helpful. Here's how to make it so in your thinking and writing.

> Recall discussions you've had about the subject, particularly discussions with people who don't share your view. Consider what they said on those occasions and what those statements suggest they would say in response to your present position.
>
> Recall the views you have heard expressed about the issue on television talk shows, in books, newspapers, and magazines, and even in soap opera dialogue. Focus on arguments that oppose yours. Consider where and how those arguments would most likely arise in response to your position.

NINE COMMON REACTIONS

Speculating about your readers' reactions to your position on the basis of your previous reading and listening, though an excellent way to anticipate those reactions, is not the only way. You can also consider the most common reactions to any argument about an issue, the reactions that occur not because of the particular nature of the subject, but because of the weaknesses of human discourse. Those reactions, which follow, are expressed in the form of questions that will occur to your readers. In each instance, one or more suggestions are given for answering the question and thus refining your composition.

1. *What is the meaning of this passage?* This question will arise whenever one of your statements is vague or ambiguous (open to more than one meaning), or when you use a technical term not familiar to your audience. Rephrase vague or ambiguous statements to express exactly what you mean. Define all technical terms or terms you are using in a sense your readers might misunderstand.
2. *What is the relevance of this statement to the issue under discussion?* Not every idea you think of will be relevant to the issue you are examining. Accordingly, there is always the possibility that an irrelevant idea will escape your scrutiny and find its way into your composition. Moreover, some ideas that are relevant will not appear so to your readers unless you make their relevance clear. For example, a student was presenting his argument against the awarding of "palimony" (alimony payments for people who lived together without benefit of marriage). He included this sentence in his composition: "Many marriages do not last because the people involved lack the maturity necessary to make them

work." Since the relevance of this statement to the issue of palimony is not self-evident, and the writer provided no clarification, his readers were very likely confused. Whenever you find any statement in your writing whose relevance is not clear, either provide the necessary explanation or delete it from the composition.

3. *How does this idea relate to what the author said earlier? Are the ideas compatible?* Unless you scrupulously follow your plan when you write your composition, you may say something in the fourth paragraph that contradicts, or at least appears to contradict, what you said in the second paragraph. When that happens, readers who oppose your position will be inclined to regard the error as proof that you are a careless thinker and dismiss your entire presentation. For example, a student was advancing the idea that there should be no special penalty for missing college classes; that is, that not handing in assignments should be penalized, but mere absence should not. She made that position clear in paragraph one. Then in paragraph three she wrote, "I realize that there are cases in which attendance is a legitimate marking factor, such as physical education, which centers around activity performance, and courses in which class participation is expected." Since class expectations are determined by the professor, the last part of her sentence can only mean that attendance counts whenever the professor wants it to, and that idea contradicts her main idea.

   Whenever you find two or more statements in your composition that are or appear to be inconsistent with one another, revise one or more of them to achieve consistency.

4. *Why does the author believe this? What is his or her basis for asserting it?* This question will arise whenever you state your view about a disputed matter yet neglect to explain why you find that view preferable to some other view. The question often arises with amateur writers because they tend to present their judgments but omit the reasoning that underlies those judgments. For example, an amateur writer will state, "I believe that our society will soon take a more conservative view of morality" and then move on to another point, never realizing that her or his readers will be left wondering "What makes the author believe this rather than believing that society's view of morality will stay the same or grow more liberal?"

   Such unsupported assertions often occur when the point of discussion is what *should be,* perhaps because people often have strong convictions in such matters and thus find it easier to pretend that their assertions are beyond questioning. "Money should never be pursued as an end in itself," "The United States should lower its tariffs on imported goods," "The speed limit on interstate highways should be raised to 75," and "This college should raise its admissions standards" are examples of assertions of what should be.

Whenever you make any assertion your readers are likely to question, and you fail to explain the basis for that assertion, you do yourself a disservice. However sound the reasoning that led you to your conclusion, it will not persuade your readers unless you present it. Conclusions by themselves are unpersuasive.

5. *What evidence does the author have that the problem is as serious or significant as stated, or that the solution proposed is effective?* This question is related to the previous one; both arise from an author's excessive reliance on assertion. Yet it differs from the previous question in that it challenges, not the omission of the reasoning that underlies the judgment, but the omission of the data that demonstrate the relationship between the judgment and reality. Persuasive writers are sensitive to the need for evidence to support their assertions; they know that critical readers, particularly readers who do not share their view, will not accept their assessments of reality without some kind of documentation that those assessments are accurate.

For this reason, persuasive writers assign more space in their writing to *showing* than to *telling*. Whenever they make a statement like "The rise in teenage pregnancies over the last decade has been dramatic," they follow it with statistics to document its correctness. Whenever they write a sentence like "Many states are beginning to treat criminals more harshly," they offer examples to show that this is so—for example, specific changes in the criminal code in several states, more stringent rules for plea bargaining, fewer suspended sentences. Whenever they say "Many people are convinced" or "Numerous authorities have said," they mention specific people and explain what they said and where and when they said it.

In providing such evidence in your writing, keep in mind that real examples are usually more persuasive than hypothetical (made-up) examples. No matter how plausible a hypothetical example may be, readers may still wonder why, if the problem is as serious as you say it is or the solution is so effective, you are not able to cite a real case to support your assertion.

6. *Is the evidence cited by the author representative? Are the situations he or she presents typical?* It is not enough to support your assertions with evidence; the evidence you use must also cover at least the most common situations that can be expected to develop. If, for example, you were arguing that students should not be penalized for missing college classes and you cited examples of unavoidable absence—varsity athletes attending out-of-town games, for instance, and cases of hospitalization—your readers might well ask whether those cases were representative of student absence in general. "What about cases where students miss class irresponsibly?" they might ask. Whenever you find that you have been too selective in choosing your evidence and have ignored examples that do not support your view, revise your paper to make your evidence more representative of reality.

7. *What is the significance of the author's treatment? Are there any important historical elements the author has omitted?* The most brilliant solution will be unimpressive to readers who don't understand the nature and background of the problem. For example, if you were presenting an argument in favor of teaching creative thinking in grade and high school classes, your readers might be unaware that creative thinking is not taught at present in most schools, what specific value creative thinking can have in various careers, and what historical developments have prevented the acceptance of creative thinking (or for that matter critical thinking) as a legitimate teaching objective. Wherever the probability exists that your readers will not appreciate the significance of your ideas because they lack the necessary understanding to see them in historical context, provide appropriate explanations.

8. *What is the implication of this statement? Does that implication make sense?* This question arises when you say something that implies something else and you fail to discuss the implication adequately. For example, in presenting your view that pornography involving children should be outlawed, you may say "Childhood is a state of innocence, so society should establish special safeguards to protect children from those who would prey on them." The implication of this statement is that a state of innocence leaves one extraordinarily vulnerable. Unless you recognize that implication and present some evidence that it is so, you will run the risk of having your readers miss the point, or worse, see it and reject it.

Of course, not every implication will withstand scrutiny as well as this one does. In discussing the problem of selling liquor to minors, for example, you may make the following statement: "There is never any excuse for selling liquor to minors, so offenders should be prosecuted without exception." The implication here is that anyone who sells liquor to minors knows that he or she is doing so. That is not a reasonable idea. Given the various ways in which identification can be forged, and the fact that many teenagers look older than their years, there must be circumstances in which an honest, law-abiding seller may be duped. (In this case you should revise your statement sufficiently that the unreasonable implication is eliminated).

9. *Does the idea apply in all cases? If it were applied, would it produce any undesirable effects?* Often an idea will apply in most cases, but not in all. Similarly, an otherwise good idea may produce certain undesirable effects. It may seem that the wisest course of action is to pretend that the imperfections don't exist, but as a rule it is far better to obey the demand of honesty and admit the unpleasant reality. If you can think of ways to extend the application of the idea to a broader range of cases, by all means do so. And if by altering the idea you can minimize the undesirable effects without diminishing the desirable ones, make that alteration. However, if you cannot, then state that fact and make the case for your idea, not on the basis that it is flawless, but on the basis that it is the best one possible.

WRITING TIP: BUILD A BALANCED CASE

Considering the questions readers may raise about your position will help you be thorough in your presentation, but it may also make you defensive about your position, and defensiveness may in turn prompt you to multiply your arguments and overwhelm your readers. When that happens you diminish your chances of being persuasive. All the insights gained in philosophy and psychology about the nature of argument and the responses of the human mind to various appeals underline the importance of this principle: *Persuasion is more likely to occur when the writer's case is balanced than when it overwhelms the readers.*

A balanced case has three characteristics. First, it is forceful, but never overwhelming. That is, it omits none of the important points you wish to make, no matter how delicate the issues being raised; but neither does it include a lot of unnecessary secondary points that beat the readers down and make them feel you are rejecting them and their position totally.

Second, a balanced case begins (as we noted briefly in Chapter 5) on a point of agreement. The psychological value of this approach is difficult to overstate. When you launch right into disagreement with your readers, you put them on the defensive. This often makes it difficult for them to respond favorably to later points, no matter how reasonable those points may be. On the other hand, when you begin on a point of agreement, you establish at the outset that you are attempting a balanced presentation and that the readers need not be defensive. This approach invites readers to give your views a fair hearing. And most honest, open-minded readers will respond that way.

Finally, a balanced case is fair, generously conceding points to the opposing side of the argument whenever it is reasonable to do so. When the issue is controversial and you feel strongly about your position, you will not wish to concede anything. Nevertheless, it is important that you do so because a controversial issue is by definition a matter on which intelligent and perceptive people are divided. In such matters it is highly unlikely that all valid points are on one side. If you refuse to get beyond narrow-mindedness and unwillingness to acknowledge the complexity of the issue and the merits of the opposing side, you have no right to expect your readers to be open-minded and reasonable in assessing your position. And if you dismiss their position lightly, or ridicule it, or misrepresent it, you should not expect them to respond differently to yours.

Before preparing the final draft of your composition, always check to be sure that you have raised and answered all relevant questions about your position and that you have made your case a balanced one by resisting the tendency to overwhelm your readers, beginning on a point of agreement, and generously conceding whatever it is reasonable to concede.

SAMPLE COMPOSITION

Here, together with the dialogue that prompted it, is a composition illustrating the persuasiveness of a balanced case.

The Dialogue

PAULA: I'm delighted to see that the idea of discipline is returning to education. I hope corporal punishment returns, too. It's really needed in the schools.

KEN: Do you mean that you'd actually approve some teacher's hitting your kids?

PAULA: If they did wrong, yes.

KEN: If a teacher ever laid his hands on my kids, I'd break both his arms.

PAULA: I see. You're opposed to violence on principle and you're ready to defend your belief with your fists. Very logical.

The Composition

The Case for Sparing the Rod

Among the suggestions for improving the nation's schools that virtually every educational commission in recent years has advanced is that discipline be restored. Learning simply cannot take place

Here the writer shows understanding of the readers' position and begins on a point readers will agree with.

when the environment is disorderly and students are permitted to ignore the rights and needs of others. This new emphasis on discipline has revived an old issue: Just how effective is corporal punishment and would its use improve the learning environment?

Past discussions of this issue have not always been pleasant. The sides of the dispute are sharply divided. One reason for this is that it is only relatively recently in history that a distinction has been made between discipline and punishment. According to Lloyd Saxton in *The Individual, Marriage, and the Family,* the two were considered synonymous until the late nineteenth century. It is therefore understandable that the association between them continues to be strong. Nevertheless, he points out, the two concepts are not the same. Discipline means "setting limits on behavior and inducing wanted behavior," whereas punishment means "deliberate infliction of pain or discomfort." Students need discipline to function in a world of other people with conflicting wants and needs. They do not, however, need punishment, though the circumstances may require it.

In this paragraph the writer presents evidence from an authority—the important distinction between discipline and punishment—that will help readers see the controlling idea in a more favorable light.

Is punishment effective? Only if it meets several conditions, according to Saxton, one of the most important being that it not evoke such emotional reactions as resentment. An experience of my own will illustrate the importance of this condition. When I was ten years old, I was forced to submit to a vigorous (though not brutal) spanking at the hands of my grade school principal. I have long since forgotten the offense that prompted this treatment. It may have been sassing the teacher or refusing to obey some rule. (I have no reason to believe I was innocent of the charge.) But though I no longer remember what I did wrong, I vividly remember how I reacted to the spanking. I cursed the principal under my breath, resolved to be even more defiant in the future, and fantasized about growing up and getting even with him. In fact, as I write I realize that I still have negative feelings toward him. I am sure that was not the effect he intended the punishment to have.

Here the writer presents important evidence from personal experience, evidence that turns the readers' attention from punishment in general to corporal punishment.

Note carefully the final sentence of this paragraph ("I am sure that . . ."), which reveals the significance of the evidence to the issue being discussed.

Resentment seems to be a common reaction to corporal punishment. That is understandable. Even when it is carried out without anger and with

This paragraph and the paragraph that follows it present the writer's analysis

reasonable restraint, and with the demands of teaching or running a school there is always the risk that it will not be, it is a humiliating experience. Moreover, it conveys just the message today's young people do not need to receive: that the way to handle problems is through physical violence. That is the message they have received every day of their lives in movies and television shows, in popular music, on the evening news, and sometimes in the streets they walk. And it is a message that brutalizes.

of corporal punishment and explain why the writer rejects it.

Teachers have a special reason to reject corporal punishment. They represent a profession that emphasizes rational processes over irrational processes, and positive responses to problems over negative responses. Where punishment is necessary, they should prefer to assign students activities that are in some way constructive. For example, where things have been broken, students can be made to repair them; where walls have been defaced, they can be directed to clean or repaint them. In cases where such assignments are not appropriate, there are many alternatives, such as assisting the school custodians or librarians, doing community service at a local hospital or civic center, reading to the residents of a home for the elderly, and researching and writing a paper on the concept of kindness, or cooperation, or the dignity of the human person.

In brief, the case against corporal punishment in the schools is not that it is terrible or that its effect is traumatic, but that it is inappropriate and ineffective. There are better ways to reform student behavior.

The conclusion is a clear, direct statement of the idea implicit in the previous three paragraphs.

DIALOGUE EXERCISES

Analyze each of the following dialogues as you did the dialogues in previous chapters. (Be sure to investigate any issue for which you lack sufficient information to make an informed judgment.) Anticipate your readers' reactions and refine your position. Then write a composition on one of the dialogues, presenting and supporting your view of the issue and applying the writing tip given at the end of the chapter.

1 ______________________________

Note: According to the U.S. Census Bureau, a woman who is eighteen in 1983 who earns a bachelor's degree will earn, in her working lifetime, less than half what a male college graduate will make, and 40 percent less than what a male with only a high school diploma will make.[1]

ALEXIS: That's positively outrageous. And they say that women have made such great gains over the past decade.

CARLOS: Before you get carried away, admit one thing: There must be a reason for the gap. Maybe the projection is based on the idea that women won't work every year, that they'll spend half their lives staying home and raising children. Or that they'll choose part-time over full-time employment when they get married.

ALEXIS: I don't buy it at all. But even if that were true, it doesn't explain the difference between female college graduates and male high school graduates.

CARLOS: There could very well be an explanation for that, too. Many male high school graduates enter skilled trades, where salaries are naturally higher than white-collar salaries. Women probably don't go into trades. So you see, Alexis, you can't seize upon every statistic as evidence that poor subjugated women are being abused by a big, bad chauvinistic society. It just isn't so.

2 ______________________________

Note: A report in Highwire, *the national student magazine, says that every year in the United States, 500,000 teenagers are thrown out of their homes. The average age of those teenagers is sixteen, and they often turn to prostitution, drug dealing, and other crimes to support themselves on the streets.*[2]

JULES: Any parent who would throw a teenager out of the house should be horsewhipped. When you bring a human being into the world you have an obligation to care for him or her until age twenty-one.

SHEILA: You're being much too hard on parents. I'm sure there are parents who try their best but finally decide they can't get through to their teenagers and tell them to leave.

JULES: That's a contradiction. If they tried their best, there wouldn't be a problem. Kids don't rebel without a reason. When parents care for them and give them understanding and love, they respond in kind.

SHEILA: But what about cases where the kids flatly refuse to follow reasonable rules, steal from their parents, and misuse their home? Then parents may have no alternative. I've heard of cases where kids actually abuse their parents physically.

JULES: I'm not sure I believe that ever happens, but if it does, I'm sure it happens very infrequently. It's hardly typical.

3 ____________________________________

APRIL: Have you ever felt that your life was empty, that it lacked meaning?

JUNE: Yes, but when that happens I tell myself that I'm not busy enough. I find that when I have some purpose for a particular block of time—an hour, a day, a week—such feelings simply don't occur to me.

APRIL: Oh, you're just not very philosophical, that's all. If you were, you'd understand what I mean. If you were an existentialist, you'd know.

JUNE: I admit I never studied philosophy, and that includes existentialism. Still, I have a good understanding of myself. Now you can say I am odd, but I believe sitting around speculating about the meaning of my life is wasting my life.

APRIL: That's foolish. How can a life be wasted?

JUNE: Why can't it be? If a minute can be wasted, an hour can be wasted, then why not a life, which is nothing more than an accumulation of minutes and hours?

APRIL: You seem so sure of yourself. How do you know that your life adds up to anything, that it transcends the mundane?

JUNE: I guess I don't really know. All I try to do is use my time wisely, to spend it on activities I think are important, to set goals and work towards them.

APRIL: Forgive me for saying it, but sometimes you talk like an intellectual peasant.

4 ____________________________________

JACQUELINE: At last, after several decades of trying, the advocates of aid to private and parochial schools have a chance of winning the fight for tuition tax credits.

HECTOR: If they do, it will mean the end of public education in America.

JACQUELINE: I can see you've succumbed to the scare psychology of the public school propagandists. There's nothing dangerous about aid to private schools. It's a simple matter of justice. It's a free country and parents should be able to choose where their children go to school without financial penalty.

HECTOR: Where's the penalty now? If people want to send their kids to a private or parochial school, then fine, that's their right. But they should pay for it out of their own pockets and not ask for government support.

JACQUELINE: Being able to deduct the cost of education on their tax returns is not the same as receiving government support.

HECTOR: Yes it is, exactly the same. And when the schools involved are religious schools, then the government will be violating the Constitution and supporting religion.

5 ______________________________

HOLLIS: I read recently that TV cable companies can take people to court if they are receiving the cable company's signal without paying for it.

EVANGELINE: Do you mean if I hook into the line that travels right across my property and receive Home Box Office or other cable shows, I am breaking the law? And what if I spend a couple of thousand dollars for a big dish antenna that picks up the cable company's signal. Am I breaking the law there, too?

HOLLIS: Yes, in both cases. And they can prosecute you.

EVANGELINE: How can they prevent me from receiving a signal that's in the *air?* Does the cable company own the air? That's a bad law. I'm going to write my representatives in the state legislature and in Congress and demand that it be repealed.

6 ______________________________

RAPHAELA: The time is long overdue for a public debate over the value of compulsory education.

JUDITH: That value is self-evident. From the political standpoint, a democratic society can't survive without educated citizens. From the social standpoint, a healthy society depends on people's enlarging their capacities and making a contribution to the common good.

From the human standpoint, potential is worth little until it is realized.

RAPHAELA: That sounds good, and I really don't disagree with it. My point is that forcing kids to be in school when they don't want to be is no more effective than forcing food down the throat of someone who doesn't want to eat. Compulsory education is largely responsible for all the disciplining and punishing that exists in the schools.

JUDITH: What would you replace compulsory education with?

RAPHAELA: With a proposal I read about recently. In that plan every citizen would be offered a total of twelve years of public education that could be taken at any time during his or her life. Thus people could drop out of school at age ten or fourteen or sixteen and return ten or twenty years later to complete their education at a time when they were ready and eager to learn.[3]

7 ______________________________

HERSCHEL: I feel sorry for those people who have children or spouses in religious cults. They don't know whether their loved ones will come to their senses and return home or remain strangers to them. It's a terrible thing to have someone you love completely and suddenly reject you because of allegiance to a religion you never even heard of.

JOYCE: I think the right answer is to kidnap them from the cult and have them deprogrammed. A lot of people have resorted to that.

HERSCHEL: I can understand why, but I don't think that approach is right. After all, the people are being made to come home against their will. That is a violation of their rights.

JOYCE: But they were brainwashed by the cult leader, so any decision they made to remain in the cult was made under duress. That fact justifies the drastic response of kidnapping and deprogramming. Anyway, you can't expect people to see their loved ones' lives thrown away out of fanaticism, whether it bears the name of religion or not.

8 ______________________________

Note: In early 1983 the government issued a 1323-page report on human rights practices in 162 countries. The study detailed not only living conditions, but also political oppression, killings, and torture in virtually every country in the world. Many of the countries where serious human rights violations were found maintain diplomatic relations and conduct trade with the United States.[4]

LUDWIG: The United States should sever diplomatic relations with any country that grossly violates the basic human rights of its citizens. In addition, the government should ban all U.S. trade with the country.

EVE: We have no business telling other sovereign countries what to do. We certainly wouldn't let them tell us what to do. Why should we presume to tell them?

LUDWIG: We don't commit atrocities or deny our citizens their basic rights, so our situation is not comparable.

EVE: Besides, what good would it do to alienate those countries? It would only drive them closer to the communist bloc nations. If we continue to have relations and trade with them, we can over the years persuade them to outgrow their repressiveness.

LUDWIG: How can we stand for human rights if we don't stand against human rights violations? If we try gentle persuasion over the years, hundreds of thousands of people will suffer before any change is made, and we will have their blood on our heads.

9 ______________________________

BABETTE: Sebastian, do you approve of euthanasia?

SEBASTIAN: Do you mean "mercy killing"?

BABETTE: Yes.

SEBASTIAN: No, I don't. It leaves a person's life at the mercy of people who may have other interests than his or her well-being: for example, the doctor who has received an urgent request for a heart, or liver, or kidney and wishes to hasten the person's death to meet that request; or the relatives of a terminally ill patient who are lusting after his or her estate.

BABETTE: I approve of it. It not only spares terminally ill patients pain and suffering but saves their families the staggering medical expense of long-term intensive care and protracted grief.

SEBASTIAN: A person's life is a sacred and precious thing—too much so to be ended by other people, no matter how well-intentioned or merciful they are. As a matter of fact, I believe it is too precious for the person himself or herself to assign others the right to pull the plug.

10 ______________________________

Note: When Elizabeth Taylor learned that a TV movie based on her life was in preparation, she went to court to block its production, claiming that the so-called docudrama was "simply a fancy new name for old-fashioned invasion of privacy, defamation, and violation of an actor's rights."[5]

SOLOMON: Good for Elizabeth Taylor. The courts should support her. What right do writers or producers have to tell her life story, fictionalized or otherwise? It's her life.

JEROME: If that were the case, then biographies would be outlawed unless they were "official, approved" versions, and such versions are usually self-serving at best.

SOLOMON: This is not a case of biographical writing. It's fiction, so it's bound to have scenes that the writer has made up out of his or her imagination. Such scenes could defame Taylor.

JEROME: There has been so much reporting about her life that there's little chance left of defaming her.

SOLOMON: Still, it's possible, and she should be protected against it.

JEROME: She is protected. She can sue for damages after the movie is shown. That's very different from preventing it from being shown, which is censorship.

More Dialogues for Critical Thinking and Writing

THE DIALOGUES in this section are designed to challenge your composite skill in critical thinking and to test your mastery of all the techniques and strategies detailed in the chapters. Longer and more complex than most of the dialogues you have seen so far, they present the wide range of problems found in everyday conversation. Be prepared to encounter irrelevant material, unfocused issues, errors in reasoning, blurred distinctions, and unwarranted assumptions, as well as a modest assortment of insights and even an occasional creative idea. In many cases you may have to withhold judgment until you have investigated the issues in some depth.

As you analyze the dialogues and express your judgments, be sure to use the thinking strategy and follow the writing guidelines presented in the preceding chapters. To assist you in doing so, here are a summary of that strategy and a list of those guidelines:

A Thinking Strategy

1. Control your bias.
2. Understand each side of the issue.
3. Analyze each side for errors and assumptions.
4. Investigate, as necessary, to accumulate evidence.
5. Evaluate the evidence.
6. Form a judgment.
7. Refine your position.

Writing Guidelines

Plan your composition before writing it.

Select a controlling idea and use it to guide you in writing.

Have a specific purpose, a clearly stated goal you wish to achieve with your readers.

Support your position with evidence.

Clarify your distinctions and the logical relationships among your ideas.

Stimulate your readers' interest.

Express your judgment carefully and keep the emphasis on *your* judgment.

Be sensitive to your readers' needs and build a balanced case.

Be exact and economical in your expression.

Make your writing lively.

Break your thoughts into paragraphs.

Use standard punctuation and observe the conventions of spelling, grammar, and usage.

Revise your rough draft.

Review the summary and list from time to time so that you don't overlook an important step or guideline consideration. If you wish, use them as a checklist as you deal with each issue.

DIALOGUE EXERCISES

1 ______________________

VIRGINIA: War is the greatest scourge of humankind. We'd all be better off if all the weapons were dismantled or destroyed.

HANNIBAL: A pretty sentiment, but hopelessly idealistic. War has been with us since earliest recorded history, and probably before that. There's little chance for it to be eliminated.

VIRGINIA: How can you be so casual about it? It threatens every living creature. The superpowers have enough destructive power at their disposal to kill every living thing on earth many times over.

HANNIBAL: I'm not casual, just realistic. War is a necessary evil. When an aggressor invades a country, the people have the choice of submitting or resisting. The only effective resistance is through combat, through war.

VIRGINIA: But modern warfare is more than effective resistance. It's no longer a case of soldier killing soldier. Since the bombing of Dresden, London, Hiroshima, and Nagasaki during the second world war, hundreds of thousands of innocent noncombatants have been killed. There's no justification for that.

HANNIBAL: Such events are tragedies, I agree. But what alternatives did we have? What alternatives do we have? Should we allow ourselves to be enslaved by our enemies? To do that would be to dishonor all that our country stands for and disgrace the memories of all those who loved freedom enough to die for it.

VIRGINIA: "My country right or wrong," huh? Well, I don't buy it. I think we have a higher obligation to humanity than to our country. First we should work for a mutual freeze with the Soviets. But if that fails, we should show them we are sincere in our desire for peace and disarm ourselves unilaterally.

HANNIBAL: That would play nicely into their hands. The Soviets are not like us, as difficult as that may be for you to believe. They are bent on domination. They have said time and again, "We'll bury you." Your spineless philosophy would hand them the shovel.

2 ______________________________

Note: In August 1983, the American Bar Association approved a code of ethics that included the provision that a lawyer who learns of client wrongdoing must avoid helping his or her client and should both withdraw from the case and inform those who might be affected by the misdeed.[1]

BARNABY: Absurd. Such a code changes the nature of the lawyer-client relationship. Historically, lawyers have been regarded like members of the clergy: whatever their clients told them was treated in confidence. Now clients will be unable to confide in their attorneys for fear they will be betrayed to the authorities.

FERNANDO: I support the change. It only corrects what has been an outrageous situation in American law. Lawyers have been so single-minded in their defense of clients that they have often been, in effect, enemies of the public and accomplices in crime.

BARNABY: That is a terrible slander. It maligns an entire profession.

FERNANDO: I stand by what I said. Think for a moment about all the legal manipulating that has been done by lawyers to find some loophole to get their clients off. All that energy, all that intellect and imagination dedicated to freeing criminals who then go right back out and prey on other people. It shouldn't be that way.

BARNABY: It has to be that way. There's no other way to ensure everyone's right to a fair trial.

FERNANDO: You're mistaken. The British system of law certainly honors the concept of a fair trial. And yet lawyers in that system have an obligation not exclusively to their clients, but to *society* as well. That is precisely what the new code of ethics will accomplish.

BARNABY: What it will accomplish is to leave the individual helpless against the awesome power of the state. The Constitution will cease to be a working document.

3 ______________________________

AUDREY: How can people in this country live as well as they do when there is so much poverty in the world?

IRVING: Not everybody in this country lives that well.

AUDREY: Even the poor in this country are well-off by Asian or African standards. And the middle and upper classes live at a level most people in those continents literally couldn't conceive of in their wildest dreams.

IRVING: It's sad, but it's reality and there's no way to do anything about it.

AUDREY: There certainly is. We could start by dividing the wealth in our own country more equitably. We could wipe out poverty almost overnight. And then we could begin sharing with the poorest of the poor nations of the world.

IRVING: Slow down a bit. Just how would you get the wealthy to agree to give away their wealth? Don't you think they'd object? And even if by some magic you did accomplish that, how would you overcome the massive obstacles to global sharing?

AUDREY: Of course, I don't expect all the rich people would willingly share their wealth. They didn't get rich by being generous. I'd fight for legislation to make it mandatory. . . .

IRVING: Now you're talking socialism.

AUDREY: Labels don't scare me. If my idea eliminates hunger and poverty, then I don't care if you call it socialism, or communism, or even satanism. After all, what's in a name?

IRVING: But your crazy idea *wouldn't* work. It would only start a class war here with the rich aligned against the poor. No one would gain. Everyone would suffer.

AUDREY: If that's what it takes, then so be it. No one deserves to live in luxury while another starves to death. That is basic to all religion and all morality.

4 ___

Note: Shirley MacLaine is best known as a movie actress. But she is also an author. In her latest book she maintains that she lived a number of former lives. She claims, for example, to have once lived as a male teacher who committed suicide on the lost continent of Atlantis.[2]

CLAUDIA: That's nutty. She must be pretty desperate for publicity to spout such drivel.

JANET: She's very serious about her belief, and she's not alone in it.

CLAUDIA: How can anyone this side of bananas believe she lived other lives?

JANET: Haven't you ever had the déjà vu experience, knowing that you've been somewhere or experienced something before, even though you are certain you've never been there or experienced it?

CLAUDIA: Yes, I have, but what has that to do with reincarnation?

JANET: Reincarnation is a belief that helps a person make sense out of such strange experiences. Stop to think about it objectively for a moment. Those experiences may be faint memories of former lives.

CLAUDIA: And how does the idea of death fit into that belief?

JANET: Death is not the end of life. It's only the end of the soul's habitation in a particular body. The soul never dies—it merely leaves the body and migrates to the astral plane.

CLAUDIA: The what?

JANET: The astral plane. I'm not sure I understand it myself, so I can't explain it well. I believe it's a different level of existence. It's not part of the material world, and not part of space as we know it. Rather, it's a kind of other dimension.

CLAUDIA: Where is it located?

JANET: It has no place, if I understand it correctly. It just is.

CLAUDIA: After hearing more about reincarnation, I'm even more convinced that it's drivel, pure and simple. It's amazing to me that so many people have given up traditional Western religion—Catholicism, Protestantism, and Judaism—because they find it hard to believe, and then they embrace kooky religions that are *impossible* to believe. Who was it that said "It's impossible to underestimate people"?

JANET: It's really not nonsense, believe me. It's just that I can't do it justice in my explanation.

5 ______________________________

HILARY: Do you know that business about "inalienable rights" in the U.S. Constitution?

BRUCE: It's not in the Constitution—it's in the Declaration of Independence. And it's not "inalienable rights." That's the modern expression. The Declaration says "unalienable rights."

HILARY: I don't need a history or language lesson, Bruce. You know what I mean.

BRUCE: Yes, I do. What about it?

HILARY: I don't buy it, that's what. What it says isn't so.

BRUCE: It says "We hold these truths to be self-evident, that all men are created equal, that they are endowed by their Creator with certain unalienable rights, that among these are Life, Liberty and the pursuit of Happiness." What can you possibly challenge about that?

HILARY: To begin with, the notion that God gives people rights. That's an outmoded notion. Even if God exists, we know today that it's society that grants individuals their rights. Second, the notion that people's rights are inalienable . . .

BRUCE: That means they can't be taken away.

HILARY: Don't interrupt. I know what it means. And that's just the point. They can be taken away. What society gives, society can take away. It's as simple as that. But if you need further proof, I give you Russia, Poland, Cuba. I could extend the list indefinitely. All those countries deny people certain rights. That proves that no rights are inalienable.

BRUCE: True, society can and often does take people's rights away, but when that happens, it is wrong.

HILARY: Not so. What about abortion? No one can deny that a fetus is alive. Abortion takes away that life, and the law permits that to happen. And what about capital punishment? The state takes criminals' lives because of the seriousness of their crimes. So much for the inalienable right to life.

BRUCE: But the cases you cite are special cases. The circumstances are unusual.

HILARY: That's totally irrelevant. The circumstances differ in virtually every individual case. That's what makes cases individual. Now let me continue. The last two so-called inalienable rights fare little better when we consider the real world. People are granted liberty and the pursuit of happiness as long as they do and pursue things society deems acceptable. They aren't free to bet on a college football game or drive their cars seventy-five miles an hour without risking arrest. Nor are they free to pursue happiness, let's say in the form of sex, if their sexual preferences are too wide of the norm.

BRUCE: Everything you've said is positively subversive of the American way. It is nothing less than a frontal assault on the underlying principles of democracy. I'd expect that of a communist, but not of someone who claims to be an American.

HILARY: I don't believe it's un-American to state the truth. But if it is, then so be it. I'd rather be un-American than a hypocrite.

6 ______________________________

LUCIUS: Did you hear about the local high school board? They banned several books from the school library. Salinger's *Catcher in the Rye* was one. And Vonnegut's *Slaughterhouse Five* was another. If I remember correctly, they even banned Steinbeck's *Grapes of Wrath*. That kind of self-righteous behavior makes my blood boil.

NADINE: Why? What's wrong with people on the school board doing what they think is right? Isn't it their job to make such decisions?

LUCIUS: It would be OK if they made the decisions on their own. But there was a large pressure campaign by a local group, Citizens for Sticking their Noses into Other Peoples' Business, or some such name. I object to that kind of group's pressuring the school board.

NADINE: Didn't you sign the nuclear freeze petition last week? What's the difference between your voicing your objection to the nuclear arms race and their voicing their objection to certain books?

LUCIUS: It's not the same thing at all. I have a right to object because my tax dollars are being spent on an insane weapons race.

NADINE: And their taxes are being spent to buy library books that they regard as harmful.

LUCIUS: It's not for them to say what books are harmful. For that matter, it's not for the school board to say.

NADINE: Then who should say?

LUCIUS: The teachers and the teachers alone. They are the ones with the expertise to decide what's relevant to education and what's not, what is literature and what is trash.

NADINE: It doesn't take a college degree to recognize garbage. Besides, teachers are human—they can make mistakes. I don't see why parents should be expected to sit silently by while their children are being assigned material that challenges the values they, the parents, brought them up to believe.

LUCIUS: Children have a right to learn. And the process of learning involves challenging the values we were brought up to believe.

NADINE: Do I understand you correctly? Are you saying it is right for the schools to challenge the values parents raise their children to honor?

LUCIUS: That's exactly what I'm saying. How can you grow intellectually if you merely accept what you've been taught? You've got to challenge, probe, doubt. That's why parents and citizens' censorship groups should keep their bright blue noses out of the schools.

7 ______________________________

BROOKE: There's a simple solution to the oppressive cost of the prison system in this country.

LOUISA: What's that—to gas all the prisoners?

BROOKE: Ha, ha, my sides are splitting. No, I'm serious. The simple solution is to have the prisoners work for their keep.

LOUISA: I'm all for that. Give them a taste of slave labor, the kind of thing the Russians are famous for.

BROOKE: I'm not talking about cutting down trees in Siberia or pounding big rocks into little ones. I'm talking about good old honest work: jobs like making furniture, assembling machines, running computers—every kind of job that's done outside prison walls.

LOUISA: Are you saying the government should compete with private enterprise?

BROOKE: Not at all. Businesses and industries would contract with the government to set up operations in the prisons. They'd run classes to teach prisoners how to do skilled jobs and they'd supervise the work.

LOUISA: Would the prisoners get paid?

BROOKE: Yes. I'd have them receive the normal pay for the job when it's done outside prison. Then I'd require them to pay for their cell, food, clothing, medical care, and so on. Whatever money was left over, they could keep.

LOUISA: You make it sound good, but did you consider the full impact of that idea on our society? It would take jobs away from honest, law-abiding citizens and increase unemployment. Besides, the company that got the prison contract would be able to produce its goods or services cheaper than the competition. In time the competition would be driven out of business and there'd be more unemployment. With the present threat to American business from foreign competition, we certainly don't need to create a new threat, especially from people who have already been convicted of preying on society.

BROOKE: But everybody concedes that prisons are failing in their main job, to rehabilitate criminals. This would help rehabilitate them. It would give them a chance to learn an honest trade, to gain some self-respect, to replace bad habits with good ones.

LOUISA: Here it comes, the liberal crap about the job of prisons being to rehabilitate. Come off it, please. The reason prisons are bulging at the seams and saddling us all with an intolerable tax burden is the country club atmosphere liberals like you have created in prisons. Prisoners don't mind returning. I say forget giving prisoners jobs; just take away their TV's and their privileges, stop feeding them gourmet food, and fewer of them will want to return when they've been released. Making prisons a punishment instead of a reward, that's the solution to the prison problem.

8 ______________________________

LEO: Do you know what's insane?

EDWINA: What?

LEO: The treatment of insane people in our legal system. If a person commits a crime and is found to be insane, or even suspected of being so, he's allowed to plead not guilty by reason of insanity. That's crazy.

EDWINA: I don't think it's crazy at all. No other handling of such cases would be fair.

LEO: Face the facts. Most of those people who plead insanity are as sane as you and I. They're taking advantage of the loophole provided by the insanity plea.

EDWINA: I grant you that some are, but not most. And besides, the psychologists and psychiatrists brought in by the courts can detect when insanity is faked.

LEO: That's what you think. I've read lots of articles about how people fooled them. As a matter of fact, I can recall a case several years ago when some people, either journalists or graduate students, did an experiment to see whether professionals could be deceived. They didn't commit a crime, naturally, but they arranged to get themselves recommended for psychiatric evaluation. Then they faked insanity and managed to fool the professional staff of the institution again and again. Ironically, only the inmates recognized that they weren't crazy.

EDWINA: All right, I'll grant that psychologists and psychiatrists make mistakes. But such cases are the exception and not the rule. The fact is that there are specific kinds of mental illness, each with its own characteristic symptoms that can be recognized. More important, when people have such an illness they are not responsible for their actions.

LEO: You mean the law has chosen, insanely, not to hold them responsible for their actions.

EDWINA: I mean exactly what I said—they are not responsible for their actions. They don't know what they're doing, their sense of right and wrong is disconnected, and they act either out of compulsion or without awareness of the nature of their actions.

LEO: How can you pick up a knife and stab someone and not know what you're doing?

EDWINA: Easy. If you become convinced that many of the people around you are not people at all, but giant salamanders bent on taking over the planet and you grab a knife and begin stabbing them to save the human race, you don't know what you are doing. More exactly, you know in your own mind that you are doing one thing, but you don't know what you are *really* doing.

LEO: But you're saying that what should count when a sane person commits a crime is what he *does,* the reality, yet what should count when an insane person commits a crime is what he thought he was doing. That's inconsistent.

EDWINA: It's not inconsistent at all. It's judging different cases differently.

LEO: And what do you say about cases of temporary insanity? Don't they strain belief just a bit? They're so convenient. "Oh, your honor, I was insane just when I did that horrible deed. Right afterward, I regained my senses."

EDWINA: I don't see how they strain belief. We all experience a variety of emotions every day. If people can lose control of their emotions, why is it so difficult to conceive of someone's losing a grasp on reality temporarily?

LEO: It's so frustrating talking to you, Edwina. I have the feeling I'm dragging an impossible load up a steep mountain.

EDWINA: Maybe the load would be lighter if you unburdened yourself of your misconceptions.

LEO: Touché. I'll make one last attempt to get you to be reasonable. Won't you agree that there's something wrong with letting people go free after they've lost their sanity and committed crimes? Wouldn't it be better for them if they were kept in an institution and made to pay in some way for the crime? And wouldn't it be better for the public to be protected against the possibility of their losing control again?

EDWINA: To keep them institutionalized as long as they are insane makes sense. But they should be released as soon as they are diagnosed as sane. To keep them in one day longer because society is afraid or wishes to punish them is unjust.

9

CHARLOTTE: I fear that by the time I'm old enough to retire, the Social Security system will be defunct. And if it is, I'll have nothing to live on.

ERSKINE: It's a shame we have to depend on such a system. In other societies, even some primitive ones, there's never a question of whether the elderly will be able to survive when their productive years are over. They are not only cared for but honored.

CHARLOTTE: That's the way it should be for us. When you think about it, it's damned unfair that it isn't that way. Parents are responsible for their children. If they fail to provide for them adequately, the law can step in and make them do so. Yet when parents grow too old to work, the children are considered to have no obligation at all.

ERSKINE: I read somewhere that it costs an estimated quarter of a million dollars to raise a child from birth to maturity.

CHARLOTTE: Does that include the cost of college?

ERSKINE: I don't really know. Even if it doesn't, though, it's a staggering figure. And that makes the situation with the elderly even worse.

CHARLOTTE: There should be a law making children responsible for their parents once the parents are too old or too ill to care for themselves.

ERSKINE: I agree wholeheartedly in the case of the elderly, but I believe the ill present a different case entirely. Medical care is so expensive today that it would be an intolerable burden to place on the family.

CHARLOTTE: But that burden is placed on the parents when they're bringing up the children. They must pay every time the children go to the doctor and if the children develop serious diseases, they often must drain their finances to pay the medical bills. Why should it be different when the parents become ill?

ERSKINE: Let me give you an actual case. My uncle is sixty years old and is suffering from cancer. His wife is a couple of years younger and has asthma and emphysema. Both have had tremendous medical bills over the past seven or eight years. My cousin Bertha is their only child. She is married and has three small children. She and her husband, a truck driver, barely make ends meet as it is. There's no way they could handle her parents' medical bills, too.

CHARLOTTE: That is a difficult situation I admit. But the principle is the same in cases of ill parents as in the case of elderly parents. If the elderly were respected by society, children would have a sense of responsibility for their parents in any situation of need, including the need that arises from ill health.

10 ______________________________

ROLAND: Our society has the highest per capita violent crime rate in the civilized world, perhaps in the uncivilized world as well. How would you explain that fact?

MAUDE: Ours is an inherently violent species. It's our nature to be violent, and nothing that we do to overcome our violent tendencies can ever be fully successful.

ROLAND: I disagree. Consider the Tasaday tribe discovered in the Philippines little more than a decade ago. They didn't even have words for violence in their vocabulary, nor was there any evidence of violence in their daily lives. If violence were inherent in human nature, as you suggest, then there would have surely been some trace of it in the Tasaday. No, violence is not inborn—it's acquired.

MAUDE: If it's acquired, then how do we get it?

ROLAND: There's no single cause, but one important one is the media. In recent years there has been an alarming increase in the number of assault, murder, and rape movies. Even worse, the crimes are shown graphically on the screen, the camera lingering over bloody corpses. Nothing is too gory to be shown—disemboweling, eye gouging, dismemberment. And such movies are not only shown in movie theaters but on cable TV, as well, often with the graphic scenes intact.

MAUDE: Filmmakers wouldn't produce such movies if people weren't watching them. But they are watching them, and the reason they are is that the films touch something deep down in their nature, their *violent* nature.

ROLAND: That's not so. The reason people watch violent films is that they are naturally curious, and nothing stimulates that curiosity as much as the sensational. People have been conditioned to demand instant gratification, and horror films provide that gratification in the form of cheap thrills.

MAUDE: And what harm do such films really do? To adapt an old saying, "No one was ever raped or murdered by a movie."

ROLAND: They condition us to respond favorably, or at least neutrally, to violence. They dull our sense of outrage. They brutalize us. And so, when we see a real assault on someone, we are more inclined to watch than to intervene. But the problem isn't only movies. Watch children's TV on Saturday morning and you'll see one violent act after another all morning long.

MAUDE: But those are just cartoons.

ROLAND: Don't say "just" cartoons. They are making an impression on children's minds, and in time they'll shape their attitudes, as well, the same way video games do. Stop and think how many video games have as the goal destroying enemy aircraft or gobbling up things. Everything is negative—destroy, tear down, never build and create. In time that emphasis inevitably takes its toll on a young mind.

11 ________________________________

HOPE: I heard there was a protest today outside the university laboratory building.

MILLARD: What was it about?

HOPE: A group of kooky do-gooders were protesting the use of animals in laboratory experiments.

MILLARD: Why do you call them "kooky do-gooders"? I'm sure they were just showing sensitivity to the plight of animals. I'm very much against the use of animals in experiments myself.

HOPE: Why? What do you have against such experiments?

MILLARD: Have you ever seen what they do to animals? They shave their heads and attach electrodes. They force their eyes open and put chemicals in them. Things like that, and worse.

HOPE: Come on, that sounds more like torture than experimentation. Why would they do such things?

MILLARD: To test their reactions. The chemicals are put in rabbits' eyes to help cosmetic manufacturers decide what cosmetics are least harmful to the human eye. That's really worth making helpless animals suffer, now isn't it?

HOPE: It sounds cruel, but they must have a good reason for doing it. Maybe they have no other way of testing the chemicals.

MILLARD: Don't be naive. They could find other ways to test products than by torturing animals. They do so because it's cheap and they don't give a damn about the animals.

HOPE: You make all lab experiments with animals seem immoral. Yet I can remember hearing somewhere that many labs use animals in tests designed to find cures for human disease. It's not all as frivolous as you make it out to be.

MILLARD: What difference does it make to the animal whether it suffers excruciating pain for one purpose or another? We have no right to use animals in any experiments. They are living creatures and they have rights.

HOPE: Animals have rights? How about rocks and trees? Do they have rights, too?

MILLARD: Animals are different, especially warm-blooded animals. Rocks and trees feel no pain. Animals do. And they care for their young, very much as we do. We have an obligation to treat them with special care.

HOPE: I can agree with you that we shouldn't cause animals pain unnecessarily. The reason, though, is not because they have rights—it's because it's an unworthy thing to do. Yet where we find it necessary to cause them pain, as in the case of research to find a cure for a disease like cancer or diabetes, then it is a different story. Ten thousand animal lives don't equal one human life. Animal suffering and human suffering are on an entirely different scale.

MILLARD: Where do we come off deciding what is necessary pain and what is unnecessary pain for animals?

HOPE: The Bible gives us that right. In the very first book of the Old Testament, the book of Genesis, it says: "Then God said, 'Let Us make man in Our image, according to Our likeness; and let him rule over the fish of the sea and over the birds of the sky and over the cattle over all the earth, and over every creeping thing. . . .' " What could be clearer than that?

12 ________________________________

DUDLEY: By the time your kids and mine get into school, a high school education will mean something.

ELMER: Why? Because the reforms they're talking about now will be accomplished?

DUDLEY: That's right. Our kids will be guaranteed an academic education: no more trade courses and watered-down courses, just college preparatory courses.

ELMER: It had better not be that way. There's nothing special about an academic education. Besides, there are many parents who don't want that kind of education for their kids. They want them to learn something practical, something they can use to make a living.

DUDLEY: There is something special about an academic education. It's the only real kind of education. I say everyone should have to take math, and science, and foreign language, and English, and social studies throughout high school. And not just the mickey mouse courses, like "The History of Detective Stories" and "Values Clarification," but demanding courses.

ELMER: Slow down for a minute. Just what does an academic program offer to students that's so special? And please don't answer in generalities. Be specific.

DUDLEY: Look, right now teachers are responsible for counseling teens with emotional problems, patrolling the halls, preventing drug abuse, advising unwed mothers. They haven't got time to do the things that count in education. When the emphasis is back on real learning, they'll be able to make academic education special again.

ELMER: You didn't answer my question. What is so special about an academic education? Why is reading Shakespeare better than reading Agatha Christie? They both give practice in reading, don't they? And what makes courses in foreign language any more valuable in later life than, say courses in business law or home economics? Most students will never have occasion to use a foreign language anyway.

DUDLEY: Shakespeare's works are classics. They offer insights into human nature and human life. Agatha Christie's books are merely entertainments. Foreign language teaches students to think as other people do, and since no two languages are exactly alike in the perspective they bring to reality, knowing more than one language expands students' experience of the world. It's the same with history and geography, math and science. They enlarge the mind.

ELMER: Maybe I'm a boor, but I find Shakespeare unreadable. I'm not questioning his greatness. But the English of his day is a foreign language today. Having to read it would make students suffer and grow frustrated, but I can't see how it would give them any great insights. How can you get insights from Portuguese if you don't understand Portuguese? And as far as the other subjects you mentioned go, I know many people with an education like the one you describe, and many of them are narrow-minded and insensitive. If an academic education enlarges the mind, they must have started with rather tiny minds.

DUDLEY: What kind of education do you think the schools should focus on if not an academic education?

ELMER: I think the emphasis should be on problem solving and decision making. Not just that, of course. I'd give basic skills a top priority. But as for the traditional courses in the social sciences, the sciences, foreign language, and literature, I'd replace them with more practical courses designed to deal directly with life in the real world. And I don't mean just home economics and shop. I mean courses that teach students to apply their imaginations, to think creatively, to conquer their own prejudices, to apply ethical principles to everyday life, to overcome obstacles.

ELMER: Sounds like more of the same courses that have substituted for real education for so long.

Appendix

Solving Grammatical Problems
A Brief Glossary of Usage

Solving Grammatical Problems

The following grammatical problems are the most common ones in student writing. In each case the problem is explained, and one or more sample errors and corrections are provided.

Comma Splice (CS)

A comma splice is the serious error of linking two main clauses with only a comma. There are several ways to correct this error:

1. Change the comma to a period and begin a new sentence.

Comma Splice	Charles committed the error known as comma splice, he linked two main clauses with only a comma.
Correction	Charles committed the error known as comma splice. He linked two main clauses with only a comma.

2. Substitute a semicolon or a colon for the comma.

Comma splice	Sally took her sister to the emergency room, Tom stayed behind to wait for the wrecker.
Correction	Sally took her sister to the emergency room; Tom stayed behind to wait for the wrecker.
Comma splice	Henry seems determined to fail, he seldom goes to class and never does any homework.
Correction	Henry seems determined to fail: he seldom goes to class and never does any homework. [Note: as this example illustrates, a colon is used instead of a semicolon if one of the main clauses amplifies or interprets the other.]

3. Add a coordinating conjunction (*and, but, or, nor, for, so,* or *yet*) after the comma.

Comma Splice	I believe her interpretation is mistaken, I'm certainly going to tell her so.
Correction	I believe her interpretation is mistaken, and I'm certainly going to tell her so.

4. Add a subordinating conjunction (such as *when, because, since, if,* or *although*) to one of the clauses so that it can no longer stand as a complete thought.

Comma Splice	I refuse to vote for him, he is incompetent.
Correction	I refuse to vote for him because he is incompetent.

Run-On Sentence (Run-on)

A run-on sentence is similar to a comma splice, except that where the latter has a comma, the run-on sentence has no punctuation at all. A run-on sentence may be corrected in the same ways as a comma splice. (See "Comma Splice.")

Sentence Fragment (Frag)

A sentence fragment is a group of words that is punctuated as if it were a sentence, but that lacks grammatical completeness—that is, it is incapable of standing alone as a complete thought. Eliminate sentence fragments by joining them to the clauses on which they depend for their meaning or by rewording them to make them grammatically complete.

Fragment	Faulty reasoning is not difficult to identify. If you know what to look for. [The "If" clause is a fragment.]
Correction	Faulty reasoning is not difficult to identify if you know what to look for.
Fragment	His voice suddenly changed pitch. Revealing that he was more excited about the challenge to his position than his words indicated. [The second clause is a fragment.]
Correction	His voice suddenly changed pitch, revealing that he was more excited about the challenge to his position than his words indicated.
Alternative Correction	His voice suddenly changed pitch. The change revealed that he was more excited about the chal-

lenge to his position than his words indicated. [In this version the fragment has been reworded to be grammatically complete.]

Lack of Subject/Verb Agreement (Agr)

A singular subject demands a singular form of the verb; a plural subject demands a plural form. Lack of agreement means the use of the wrong form of the verb.

Agreement Lacking Jim and Agnes, unlike most students in this course, refuses to consider views contrary to those they have always held. [The subject of the sentence is the plural ***Jim and Agnes,*** but the verb form ***refuses*** is singular.]

Correction Jim and Agnes, unlike most students in this course, refuse to consider views contrary to those they have always held.

Agreement Lacking Each of the arguments presented in the dialogue have merit, but each also oversimplifies. [Words like ***each*** and ***every*** are singular in meaning and demand a singular form of the verb. Though the verb ***oversimplifies*** is singular in form and therefore correct, the verb ***have*** is plural and therefore incorrect.]

Correction Each of the arguments presented in the dialogue has merit, but each also oversimplifies.

Note: Much of the confusion students experience over subject/verb agreement derives from a misunderstanding of the use of *-s* verb endings. To overcome this confusion, remember that the third person singular form of present tense verbs always ends in *-s*. That means whenever you are referring to one person or thing by name—*Horace, this argument, their stubbornness*—or by using the pronoun *he, she,* or *it,* any verb you use in the present tense must have an *-s* ending. For example, you should write "She argue*s* well" and "This class i*s* interesting."

Incorrect Pronoun Case (Case)

The most common errors in pronoun case concern the choice between *I* and *me,* and that between *we* and *us*. Use *I* or *we* if the word is serving as the subject of the sentence or as the complement following the verb *to be* in any of its forms (*am, are, was, were,* and so on). Use *me* or *us* if the word is serving as the direct object of the verb or as the object of a preposition. Here are some examples of common case errors and their correction.

Incorrect Case	Socrates and ***me*** would have made a good debating team.
Correction	Socrates and ***I*** would have made a good debating team.
Incorrect Case	The one the professor seems to call on most is ***me.***
Correction	The one the professor seems to call on most is ***I.***
Incorrect Case	This course is doing a lot to improve the critical thinking of ***we*** students. [The word in question is the object of the preposition ***of,*** so the pronoun should be in the objective case.]
Correction	This course is doing a lot to improve the critical thinking of ***us*** students.

Faulty Pronoun Reference (Ref)

Pronouns often make references back to earlier words in the sentence or words in a previous sentence. Such references are faulty when they are unclear or inaccurate.

Unclear Reference	Andy asked Tom to take his clothes out of the washing machine. [Whose clothes? The pronoun ***his*** is unclear here.]
Correction	Andy said, "Tom, please take your clothes out of the washing machine."
Inaccurate Reference	Professor Smalley tries to give every student a chance to express their opinion. [***Every student*** is singular but the pronoun ***their*** is plural.]
Correction	Professor Smalley tries to give all students a chance to express their opinions. [Note the plural form ***opinions*** is used because it is unlikely that all students will have the same opinion.]

Unnecessary Shift in Person or Tense (Shift)

Some shifts in person or tense are necessary. For example, you may be writing about scientists in general and then turn your attention to a particular individual. Or you may finish discussing a past event and begin discussing a present one. The kinds of shifts in person or tense that are objectionable are the unnecessary ones, the shifts from singular to plural or past to present tense and then back again without any good reason. If your instructor indicates that you tend to make this error, check your rough drafts carefully and revise them where appropriate to avoid unnecessary shifts.

Faulty Modification (Mod)

There are three types of faulty modification: dangling, misplaced, and squinting. A *dangling modifier* is a word, phrase, or clause expressed in such a way that its relationship to the rest of the sentence is unclear. A *misplaced modifier* is a word, phrase, or clause in the wrong position to convey the meaning intended. A *squinting modifier* is a word, phrase, or clause that can be understood to modify either the preceding or following word and therefore creates ambiguity.

Dangling Modifier When only five years old, my sister taught me how to play the piano. [Was your sister five years old?]

Correction When I was only five years old, my sister taught me how to play the piano.

Misplaced Modifier We saw the accident waiting for a taxi. [How can an accident wait for anything?]

Correction Waiting for a taxi, we saw the accident.

Squinting Modifier The friends I discuss my homework with often disagree with my view. [Does the writer discuss homework with them often or often disagree?]

Correction Often the friends I discuss my homework with disagree with my view.

Mixed Construction (Con)

Mixed construction exists whenever a sentence begins with one grammatical structure and ends with another.

Mixed Construction By proofreading your work for one specific kind of error at a time is the best way to overcome grammatical problems.

Correction Proofreading your work for one specific kind of error at a time is the best way to overcome grammatical problems.

Alternative Correction By proofreading your work for one specific kind of error at a time, you increase your chances of overcoming grammatical problems.

A Brief Glossary of Usage

Affect, Effect

Affect is a verb meaning "to influence." *Effect* can be either a verb or a noun. As a verb it means "to cause"; as a noun, its more common use, it means "a result."

> ***Correct*** Don't let her nagging ***affect*** your disposition.
>
> ***Correct*** Researchers have been unable to ***effect*** a cure.
>
> ***Correct*** The ***effect*** of his drinking has been tragic.

Amount, Number *See Number, Amount.*

As, Like *See Like, As.*

Awful, Awfully, Very *See Very, Awfully, Awful.*

Between, Among

Between is used when two persons, places, or things are involved; *among*, when more than two are involved.

> ***Correct*** There has never been any hostility ***between*** Tim and me.
>
> ***Correct*** There has never been any hostility ***among*** Tim, Ed, and me.

Can Hardly, Can't Hardly

Hardly in such expressions is synonymous with *barely*. The sense intended is therefore "I am able to, but just barely so." *Can hardly* conveys that intention. But *can't hardly* does not; it suggests inability rather than ability. For this reason, *can't hardly* is never acceptable.

> ***Correct*** I ***can hardly*** wait for the tournament to begin.

Conscience, Conscious

Conscience is a noun meaning "inner moral guide, sense of right and wrong in ethical matters." *Conscious* is an adjective meaning "mentally awake, aware."

Correct	Let your ***conscience*** be your guide.
Correct	He was the only one ***conscious*** after the accident.
Correct	Public servants must be ***conscious*** of their obligation to constituents.

Could Have, Could've, Could Of

Could have is standard English. *Could've* is an acceptable contraction of *could have* that is commonly used in speaking, but seldom in writing. *Could of* is never correct and probably results from hearing the contraction spoken, but not recognizing it as such. [Note: The same rule applies to *would have* and *should have.*]

Each Other, One Another

Each other is used in references to two people: *one another,* in references to more than two people.

Correct	John and Agnes can't stand the sight of ***each other.***
Correct	The students in my division seem to like ***one another.***

Effect, Affect *See Affect, Effect.*

Etc., &

Etc. is an abbreviation of the Latin, *et cetera,* which means "and others" or "and so forth." The symbol & is used in place of *and.* Although both are widely used in informal writing, many authorities still consider them (especially &) unacceptable in formal writing.

Fewer, Less

Fewer is used when speaking of things usually considered as individual units; *less,* when speaking of things not usually considered as individual units.

Correct	***Fewer*** people, ***fewer*** potatoes, ***fewer*** towns, ***fewer*** paper clips.
Correct	***Less*** mashed potatoes, ***less*** hostility, ***less*** sugar.

Himself, Hisself

Himself is the correct form. *Hisself* is unacceptable.

Correct	He decided to do his taxes ***himself.***

Hopefully

Many educated people object to the use of this word in constructions that express some particular person's hoping. For example, they would object to the sentence "*Hopefully,* this lecture will be more interesting than the one last week." They would prefer "I hope this lecture . . ." or "Let us hope this lecture. . . ." Nevertheless, its use is widespread and there is at least one accepted precedent for such an adverbial construction: the use of *admittedly,* as in "Admittedly, the error was mine." Therefore, it may be considered an acceptable form in most situations, but one that should be avoided when writing for a fastidious audience.

I, Me *See Me, I.*

Imply, Infer

Imply means "to suggest indirectly, to hint at." *Infer* means "to judge or conclude."

Correct	You seem to be ***implying*** that I got this job by dishonest means. I resent that ***implication.***
Correct	The essay ***infers*** that nuclear war is unavoidable. I reject that ***inference.***

Irregardless, Regardless *See Regardless, Irregardless.*

Its, It's

Its is a possessive pronoun. *It's* is the contraction of *it is.*

Correct	A dog will give ***its*** affection more quickly than a cat will.
Correct	Drink up—***it's*** closing time.

Lay, Lie

These words are both verbs. They are confused because one of the principal parts of each is the same. Remembering those principal parts is the key to overcoming confusion.

Lay means "to place or put." Its principal parts are *lay/laid/laid.*

Present tense	I ***lay*** [***am laying***] my pencil on the desk.
Past tense	Yesterday I ***laid*** my pencil on the desk.
Present perfect	I ***have laid*** my pencil on the desk.

Lie means "to rest or recline." Its principal parts are *lie/lay/lain.*

Present tense	I ***lie*** down for a nap each day at noon.
Past tense	I ***lay*** down yesterday at noon.
Present perfect	I ***have lain*** down regularly because the doctor ordered me to.

Less, Fewer *See Fewer, Less.*

Like, As

Contemporary usage, particularly in the field of advertising, has blurred the traditional distinction between these words in some constructions. Nevertheless, most educated people avoid substituting *like* for *as* when the meaning intended is "in the same manner or way that." For example, "Wowies taste good *like* dogyummies should" would be unacceptable in formal writing.

Me, I

Me and *I* are both personal pronouns. But *me* is in the objective case; and *I,* in the nominative. The most common error with these words is using *I* instead of *me* as the object of a preposition.

Correct	Bill went to the movies with Tom and ***me.*** [The word used here is the object of the preposition ***with,*** so ***me*** is correct.]
Correct	Bill, Tom, and ***I*** went to the movies. [The word used here is a subject of the sentence, not an object, so ***I*** is correct.]

Number, Amount

Use *number* when referring to persons, places, or things usually considered as individual units. Use *amount* when referring to things not usually considered as individual units.

Correct	A ***number*** of dogs, a ***number*** of seashells, a large ***number*** of cars, a small ***number*** of oilwells.
Correct	An ***amount*** of oil, a large ***amount*** of corn, a small ***amount*** of paint.

One Another, Each Other *See Each Other, One Another.*

Provided, Providing

Provided means "cared for" or "with the provision that." *Providing* means "furnishing."

Correct	He ***provided*** well for his family.
Correct	You may have the night off, ***provided*** you get someone to work in your place.
Correct	She was responsible for ***providing*** refreshments.

Reason Is That, Reason Is Because

The accepted expression is *reason is that.* Since both the word *reason* and the word *because* refer to cause, the expression *reason is because* is redundant.

Correct	The ***reason*** I am in college ***is that*** I want to learn.

Regardless, Irregardless

The prefix *ir-* and the suffix *-less* both mean "without." Therefore, *regardless* means "without regard" and *irregardless,* "without *without* regard." Because of its redundancy, *irregardless* is not accepted in modern usage.

Should Have, Should've, Should Of *See Could Have, Could've, Could Of.*

Themselves, Themself, Theirselves

Only the first form, *themselves,* is standard English. The others are never acceptable.

Then, Than

Then indicates time. *Than* introduces the second part of a comparison.

Correct	First we visited my aunt; ***then*** we went shopping.
Correct	There is no more dedicated athlete ***than*** my brother.

There, Their, They're

These words are pronounced in the same way. But *there* is an adverb indicating place, *their* is a pronoun showing possession, and *they're* is a contraction of *they are*.

Correct	***There*** she is—Miss Commercialism.
Correct	The students placed ***their*** library books in the book depository.
Correct	Al and Chris called to say ***they're*** going to be late.

To, Too, Two

To has many meanings, most of which you are familiar with. But it cannot be used as a substitute for *too,* which means "more than enough" or "also." Nor should either word be confused with *two,* which is the number between one and three.

Unique

Unique means "without parallel, one of a kind." Therefore, the words *more, most,* and *very* shouldn't be used with it. (To say something is "more unique" than something else is a contradiction; if it is unique, then no comparison can properly be made. To say something is "very unique" is redundant.)

Use, Usage

Use may be either a verb or a noun. As a verb it rhymes with *news* and means "to employ or put into service." As a noun it rhymes with *loose* and means "the employment or application of something." *Usage* is a more specialized noun whose most common use concerns language.

Correct	Be sure to ***use*** the correct tool for the job.
Correct	Contemporary English ***usage*** frowns on slang in formal writing.

Used To, Use To

The correct expression is *used to,* never *use to.* The error of using *use to* undoubtedly arises from the fact that the *d* and *t* sounds blend together when the expression is spoken.

Correct	***I used to*** be a careless driver, but I've reformed.

Very, Awfully, Awful

Very means "in high degree, extremely." *Awfully* means "extremely badly, terribly." Thus, *awfully* is really not a synonym for *very.* Still, it is an acceptable substitute in *informal* writing (and speaking). *Awful* is an adjective and should never be substituted for either *very* or *awfully.*

Always Correct	Tim is a ***very good*** tennis player.
Always Correct	Joe is an ***awful*** tennis player.
Correct Informally	Tim is an ***awfully good*** tennis player.
Never Correct	Tim is an ***awful good*** tennis player.

Who, Whom

Who and *whom* are pronouns referring to people. When the word used will be the subject of a verb, use *who.* When the verb already has a subject, use *whom.*

Correct	The man ***who*** runs the restaurant is sitting in the next booth. [***Who*** is subject of ***runs. Man*** is subject of ***is sitting.***]
Correct	The man ***whom*** I introduced Sally to last night just came in the door. [The verbs in this sentence—***introduced*** and ***came in***—already have subjects, so ***whom*** is the correct form to use.]

Word Endings

Learning to hear your writing as you proofread it will help you to avoid omitting word endings.

Ending Omitted	I have ***listen*** to him long enough.
Corrected	I have ***listened*** to him long enough.
Ending Omitted	He was very jealous of what ***belong*** to him.

Corrected	He was very jealous of what ***belonged*** to him.
Ending Omitted	I can't believe this is ***happen*** to me.
Corrected	I can't believe this is ***happening*** to me.

Would Have, Would've, Would Of *See Could Have, Could've, Could Of.*

You, One, A Person, We

Traditionally, *you* has been frowned upon in most formal writing. *One* has been preferred. For example, unless the sentence "You should never waste your breath arguing with a bigot" were addressed to a specific person, it would have been considered appropriate only in speech or informal writing. It would have been written "One should never waste his breath arguing with a bigot." Today many writers consider *one* too stilted for most writing situations. They prefer *a person* (or a more specific term, such as *a man* or *a woman*). *You* is also considered acceptable as long as it is not obtrusive or too personal in the particular context. In many writing situations, *we* offers a desirable balance between formality and casualness. There is no clear-cut rule, however, in this matter. To decide what is appropriate in a given situation, you should consider the occasion, the audience, and your purpose in writing.

Your, You're

Your is a possessive pronoun. *You're* is a contraction of *you are.*

Correct	***Your*** coat is in the hall closet.
Correct	***You're*** the only one I really care for.

Notes

Chapter 1

1. Quoted in Joseph Jastrow, *Effective Thinking* (New York: Simon & Schuster, 1931), p. 120.
2. This experiment, conducted by Solomon Asch, is discussed in Patricia N. Middlebrook, *Social Psychology and Modern Life,* 2nd ed. (New York: Alfred A. Knopf, 1982), pp. 430–1.
3. Reported on "Good Morning America," ABC News, 4 November 1982.
4. "Woman Sentenced to College . . . ," *Schenectady (New York) Gazette,* 9 October 1982, p. 9.
5. "Non-Smoker Wins Suit on Disabling by Smoke," *Binghamton (New York) Press,* 22 October 1982, p. 4A.
6. "Teen Sentenced for Covering Body" *Daily Star* (Oneonta, New York), 3 February 1982, p. 2.

Chapter 2

1. Interview in *USA Today,* 3 June 1983, p. 11A.
2. "A Call for Quality Education," *Life,* March 1981, p. 82.
3. "Bars' Ladies' Nights Called Reverse Sexism," *Binghamton Press,* 12 January 1983, p. 5B.
4. Reported on WIXT TV news, 9 December 1982.
5. "States Must Educate Illegal Alien Children," *Daily Star,* 16 June 1982, p. 1.
6. "Ex-Policeman Says Sex Shift Cost His Job," *Schenectady Gazette,* 28 August 1982, p. 14.
7. "Paternity Battle," *The New York Times,* 12 December 1982, p. 57.
8. "Murder Trial Minus Body OK'd," *Binghamton Press,* 15 December 1982, p. 10B.
9. "When 'News' Is Almost a Crime," *Time,* 21 March 1983, p. 84.

Chapter 3

1. David Egner, "Sioux Fight to Keep Black Hills Holy Land," *Binghamton Press,* 7 December 1982, p. 5A.
2. "Boy, 10, Sues Sister, 12," *USA Today,* 8 April 1983, p. 2A.
3. "Tough—But Flawed?—Alcohol Tests," *Christian Science Monitor,* 3 March 1983, p. 24.
4. "Unwed Dad Barred from Delivery Room," *Daily Star,* 14 May 1982, p. 2.
5. "Witch's Church Tax Free," *Daily Star,* 8 April 1982, p. 17.
6. "Try to Save Dog in British Waves Costs Lives of 4," *Binghamton Press,* 7 January 1983, p. 1F.
7. "Youth, 13, Jailed for Auto Offense," *Binghamton Press,* 1 February 1976, p. 2A.
8. "Pregnant Teacher Stirs Town," *Binghamton Press,* 22 December 1982, p. 1A.

Chapter 4

1. I am indebted to Jill Binker and Marla Charbonneau for this term.
2. "Court Rules Dogs Can Sniff for Drugs in Airport," *USA Today,* 21 June 1983, p. 7A.
3. "School's Out for Drug-Sniffing Dogs," *USA Today,* 28 June 1983, p. 7A.
4. "TV Fights Charges It Undercuts Reading," *Binghamton Press,* 29 November 1982, p. 1A.
5. "Alleged Killer Saw Film," *Binghamton Press,* 23 August 1982, p. 6A.
6. "Houston Cracks Down on Illegal Dogfighting," *The New York Times,* 8 November 1981, p. 58.
7. Robert E. Tomasson, "Suspect in 4 Connecticut Rapes Granted Bail Again," *The New York Times,* 7 November 1982, p. 55.
8. "Evanston, Ill., May Tax University Students," *The New York Times,* 7 November 1982, p. 33.
9. "Questioning Campus Discipline," *Time,* 31 May 1982.

Chapter 5

1. "Airline Co-Pilot Bakes on Skid Row," *The New York Times,* 23 May 1982, p. 27.
2. "Game Show Prizes Entice California Voters," *Daily Star,* 4 June 1982, p. 1.
3. "Woman Can Sue Estate of Rapist," *Daily Star,* 22 May 1982, p. 2.

4. "Woman Convicted of Making Ethnic Slur," *Daily Star,* 18 May 1982, p. 2.
5. "Lawyer Tests Daughter's C Grade in Court," *Daily Star,* 19 April 1982, p. 10.
6. "Dear Abby," *Binghamton Press,* 12 January 1983, p. 3C.
7. Ann Treneman, "Students Put the Bite on Faculty Dining Room," *Binghamton Press,* 7 February 1983, p. 1A.
8. "Fear Lack Nullifies Rape Case," *Binghamton Press,* 15 November 1982, p. 12A.
9. "Deceived Smoker Sues," *USA Today,* 30 June 1983, p. 2A.
10. "State Rules Let Gays and Crooks Adopt Children," *Binghamton Press,* 8 August 1982, p. 1A.

Chapter 6

1. "Four Jersey Students Lose Suit on Invalidated S.A.T. Scores," *The New York Times,* 5 August 1983, p. 1.
2. *USA Today,* 31 March 1983, p. 2A.
3. Arthur Miller, "Good Morning America," ABC-TV, 17 May 1983.
4. "His Word Against Theirs," *The New York Times,* 30 May 1983, Section 7, p. 4.
5. Brenda Eady, "Brake on for Teen Drivers," *USA Today,* 28 April 1983, p. 3A.
6. "High School Class Uses Human Cadavers in Lab," *Binghamton Press,* 15 December 1982, p. 2C.
7. George W. Cornell, "Americans Say Decalogue Is Still Applicable Today," *Binghamton Press,* 1 January 1983, p. 1B.
8. Karla Vallance, "This Time, the Rebel's on the Right," *Christian Science Monitor,* 27 January 1983, p. B1; also George Basler, "Student Paper Urges Theft and Graffiti," *Binghamton Press,* 25 January 1983, p. 1F.
9. Susan Heller Anderson, "The 'R' Rating—a Lure or a Barrier?" *The New York Times,* 2 May 1982, Section 2, p. 19.
10. David Bauman, "Schools Resorting to Booze Tests," *USA Today,* 4 May 1983, p. 3A.
11. "Court Exempts Presidents from Damage Suits," *Oneonta Star,* 25 June 1982, p. 1.

Chapter 7

1. John Leo, "Lemons from a Shady Dealer," *Time,* 23 May 1983, p. 60.
2. *Parade,* 12 September 1982, p. 13.
3. *Binghamton Press,* 9 February 1983, p. 6A.

4. Second edition, 1977, American Psychological Association, Washington, D.C.
5. Vernon Scott, "Husband, Wife Earn Living Fighting Devils, Demons," supplement to *Schenectady Gazette,* 16 October 1982, p. 35.
6. John Leo, "Bursting the South Sea Bubble," *Time,* 14 February 1983, p. 68.
7. "Top Subject for Teachers: Merit Pay," *USA Today,* 30 June 1983, p. 1D.
8. Harry Atkins, "Football, Hockey Are X-Rated," *Binghamton Press,* 19 December 1982, p. 6C.
9. Alexander Taylor, "Sexy Premiums," *Time,* 20 June 1983, p. 62.
10. Patricia Blake, "Going Gentle into That Good Night," *Time,* 21 March 1983, p. 85.

Chapter 8

1. "USA Snapshots," *USA Today,* 8 August 1983, p. 1B.
2. "500,000 Teens Booted from Home Each Year?" *USA Today,* 24 May 1983, p. 4D.
3. Maurice Wolfthal, "Should School Be Compulsory?" *New York Teacher,* 17 April 1983, p. 8.
4. Julia Malone, "Human Rights Report Could Touch Off Disputes Over Aid," *Christian Science Monitor,* 9 February 1983, p. 3.
5. "Elizabeth Taylor Vs. Tailored Truth," *Time,* 8 November 1982, p. 71.

More Dialogues for Critical Thinking and Writing

1. "Bar Code Urges Lawyers Not to Aid 'Wrongdoers'," *USA Today,* 3 August 1983, p. 3A.
2. Interview with Shirley MacLaine, *USA Today,* 16 June 1983, p. 11A.

Index

Abstract publications, 105
Affect, effect, 156
Agreement, point of, 123
Alertness to imperfection, 19
Almanacs, 105
Alternative arguments, 85–86
Always and *often,* 35, 40
Among, between, 156
Amount, number, 160
Analogy, faults in, 53–54
And relationships, 59–60
Anticipating reactions, 118–119
A person, 163
Appeals, irrational, 55–56
Art Index, 105
As, like, 159
Assertions
  basis for, 120–121
  distinguished from evidence, 38–39
  supported by evidence, 25
Assumptions
  identification of, 70–83
  implied, 71
  recognition of, 74–75
Attacking the person, 52–53
Authorities
  appeal to, 55
  emphasis on, 108–109
  as evidence, 100
  interviewing of, 103–104
Awful, very, 162

Background of problem, 122
Balanced case, 123–124
  exercises for, 126–132
  sample composition for, 124–126
Balanced reading, 19
Between, among, 156
Bias, control of, 19–20
Business Periodicals Index, 105
But relationships, 59–60

Can hardly, can't hardly, 156
Card catalog, 105–106
Causation, faults in, 54–55
Cause and effect
  assumption, 73
  order, 10
Certainty, qualifications of, 89
Clarifying relationships, 59–60
Comma splice, 151–152
Comparing arguments, 87
Complexity, order of, 10
Conceding points in argument, 124
Conclusions
  hasty, 56–57
  selection of, 76
Condition, qualifications of, 89
Conditioning minds, 4–5
Confirmation of details, 100
Conscience, conscious, 157
Consequences, assessment of, 87–88
Contradictions, 53
  elimination of, 120
Conviction, misunderstanding of, 72–73
Could have, could've, could of, 157
Critical reading, 18–34
Critical thinking, 133–149

Dangling modifier, 155
Details, confirmation of, 100
Dialogue exercises. *See* Exercises
Distinctions in dialogue, 35–49
Dominance in dialogue, 3

Each other, one another, 157
Editorials on File, 106
Effect, affect, 156
Effect-to-cause order, 10
Either-or thinking, 51–52
Emotion, appeal to, 55
Encyclopaedia Britannica, 104
Encyclopedia Americana, 104
Encyclopedias, 104
Errors
  common dialogue errors, 51–58
  probability of, 19
  in reasoning, 50–69
  in thinking, 5
Etc., &, 157
Evaluation of evidence, 22–23
Evidence
  assertion distinguished from, 38–39
  to conclusion order, 10
  conclusiveness of, 24
  conviction constituting, 72–73
  evaluation of, 22–23
  investigating issues, 99–116
  plan for finding, 101–102
  representativeness of, 121–122

Evidence (continued)
sample composition using, 26–28
of seriousness of problem, 121
writing tip on, 25–26
Examining ideas, 9–10
Examples, 121
Exercises
on assumptions, 78–83
for balanced case, 126–132
for clarifying relationships, 62–69
for critical thinking, 133–149
on distinction making, 43–49
emphasizing judgment, 111–116
using evidence, 28–34
on judgments, 93–98
Experience
consultation of, 102–103
other people's, 101
own experience as evidence, 100
Experts. *See* Authorities

Face-saving, 7
Facts on File, 106
Faith, appeal to, 55
Fallacy frenzy, 58–59
Familiar ideas, 7
Familiarity and validity, 39
Fatalism, 11
Faulty modification, 155
Fewer, less, 157
Focusing, 6
Form and substance, 38

Gaps in thinking, 10
Grammatical problems, 151–155

Hasty conclusions, 56–57
Himself, hisself, 158
Historical elements, 122
Hopefully, 158
Humanities Index, 105
Hypothetical examples, 121

I, me, 159
Ideas, 123
Identification
of assumptions, 70–83
of issues, 21–22
Implications
assessment of, 87–88
in statements, 122
Imply, infer, 158
Importance, order of, 10
Inconsistencies. *See* Contradictions
Indexes to periodical literature, 105
Index Medicus, 105
Infer, imply, 158
Information Please Almanac, 105
Interview authorities, 103–104
Introductions, 76
Investigating issues, 99–116
Irrational appeal, 55–56
Issues
identification of, 21–22
investigation of, 99–116
Its, it's, 158

Judging dialogue, 8
Judgments
authorities, *see* Authorities
avoidance of, 85
comparison of, 24
forming of, 84–98
modification of, 88–89
preference distinguished from, 36–37
reservation of, 89–90
Justification, 3
assumption and, 73–74

Knowledge as evidence, 102–103

Lay, lie, 159
Less, fewer, 157
Less important points, 37–38
Library information, 104–106
efficient use of, 106–107
Lie, lay, 159
Like, as, 159

Majority belief assumption, 73
Me, I, 159
Meaning of passage, 119
Memory, 6–7
Misconceptions about dialogues, 2–3
Misplaced modifier, 155
Mixed construction, 155
Moderation, appeal to, 55
Modification, faulty, 155
Modifying judgments, 88–89
More and less important points, 37–38
Motivation, 54–55

Negative stereotyping, 52
New York Times Encyclopedic Almanac, 105
New York Times Index, 105
Note taking, 107
Number, amount, 160

Objectivity, 39–40
Observation, 100–101
Often and *always*, 35, 40
Omission from dialogue, 23
One, 163
One another, each other, 157
Opinions, equality of, 2–3
Overgeneralization, 57
assumptions and, 70
Oversimplification, 24, 57–58

The People's Almanac, 105
Periodical indexes, 105
Person and idea distinguished, 36
Person or tense, shift in, 154–155
Persuasion, 123
Place, qualifications of, 89
Plato, 1
Point of agreement, 123
Position, determination of, 23–24
Predisposition, 20
Preference and judgment distinguished, 36–37
Preliminary judgments, 87
Pretending to know, 6–7

Pronouns
 faulty reference, 154
 incorrect case, 153–154
Provided, providing, 160
Psychological Abstracts, 105, 106–107

Qualifications and judgment, 89

Reactions
 anticipation of, 118–119
 common reactions, 119–123
Readers' Guide, 105
Reason is that, reason is because, 160
Reasoning
 assumptions and, 71–72
 errors in, 50–69
Refining your position, 117–132
Regardless, irregardless, 160
Relevance of statements, 119–120
Relevant and irrelevant material, 37
Representative evidence, 121–122
Research in Education, 105
Reserving judgment, 89–90
Run-on sentence, 152

Sample composition, 10–13
 for balanced case, 124–126
 clarifying logical relationships, 60–62
 for distinctions, 41–43
 for emphasizing judgment, 109–111
 with evidence supporting position, 26–28
 on judgments, 91–93
 stimulating reader interest, 77–78
Secondhand reports, 101
Selective perception, 6
Selective reading, 107
Self-deception, 5–8
Senses, trustworthiness of, 72
Sentence fragment, 152–153
Seriousness of problem, 121
Social Science Index, 105
Socrates, 1
Source record, 107
Speculation about reactions, 119
Squinting modifier, 155
Statistics, confirmation of, 100
Stereotyping, 52
Subject/verb agreement, 153
Summary, 25

Television, knowledge from, 102
Themselves, themself, theirselves, 160
Then, than, 161
There, their, they're, 161
Therefore relationships, 59–60
Thesaurus of Psychological Index Terms, 106–107
Thinking strategy, 133
Thirdhand reports, 101
THOB, 3
Time, qualifications of, 89
Titles, 76
To, too, two, 161
Tolerance, 3
Tradition, appeal to, 55

Understanding, 3
 of each side, 21
 and objectivity, 39
Unique, 161
Unwarranted assumptions, 71–75
Usage glossary, 156–163
Use, usage, 161
Used to, use to, 162
U.S. Government publications, 105

Validity and *familiarity*, 39
Very, awfully, awful, 162

Ward, Henshaw, 3
We, 163
Who, whom, 162
Word endings, 162–163
World Almanac, 105
Writing guide, 133–134
Writing tips, 9–10
 for balanced case, 123–124
 clarification of relationships, 59–60
 for distinctions, 40–41
 emphasis on judgment, 108–109
 on judgments, 90–91
 stimulating reader interest, 75–76
 unwarranted assumptions, 75–76
 using evidence, 25–26

You, one, a person, we, 163
Your, you're, 163